OF THE

END OF
APARTHEID

CAUSES AND CONSEQUENCES

CAUSES AND CONSEQUENCES

OF THE

END OF
APARTHEID

CATHERINE BRADLEY

RSVP

RAINTREE
STECK-VAUGHN
P U B L I S H E R S
The Steck-Vaughn Company

Austin, Texas

T 65024
09/01

Published by Raintree Steck-Vaughn Publishers,
an imprint of Steck-Vaughn Company

Developed by the Creative Publishing Company
Editor: Patience Coster
Designed by Ian Winton

Raintree Steck-Vaughn Publishers staff
Project Manager: Joyce Spicer
Editor: Shirley Shalit
Electronic Production: Scott Melcer

Consultant: Patricia Romero, Towson State University

Cover photo (large): South African President Nelson Mandela (left) and Second Deputy President F. W. de Klerk celebrate their inauguration May 10, 1994.
Cover photo (small): A typical scene during apartheid. This sign in Afrikaans and English indicates a Johannesburg post office entrance is for non-whites only.

Library of Congress Cataloging-in-Publication Data

Bradley, Catherine.
    End of apartheid / Catherine Bradley.
       p.   cm. – (Causes and consequences)
    Includes bibliographical references and index.
    Summary: Traces the origins of apartheid, the struggle against it, and the changes in South African society that brought about its end.
    ISBN 0-8172-4055-1
    1. Apartheid — South Africa — History — Juvenile literature.
2. South Africa — Race relations — Juvenile literature.
[1. Apartheid — South Africa.   2. South Africa — Race relations.]
I. Title.   II. Series.
DT1757.B75   1995
305.8'00968–dc20   95-17669
                                        CIP   AC

Printed in Hong Kong
Bound in the United States
1 2 3 4 5 6 7 8 9 0 LB 99 98 97 96 95

CONTENTS

INTRODUCTION

I contend that we are the finest race in the world and that the more of the world we inhabit, the better it is for the human race. Just fancy, those parts that are at present inhabited by the most despicable specimens of human beings, what an alteration there would be if they were brought under Anglo-Saxon influence.

Cecil John Rhodes, the English-speaking South African, who colonized Rhodesia in the nineteenth century and who founded the Rhodes scholarships.

On May 10, 1994, one of the world's most unjust and discriminatory regimes came to an end. In South Africa, the system of apartheid – or the total separation of peoples according to the color of their skin – had for more than forty years been the official policy of the ruling white minority. Pronounced "apart-hate," the word apartheid means "apartness" in Afrikaans, the language of the majority of South African whites. From 1948 the policy of apartheid had been written into the statute book of that country. By the late 1980s this resulted in a white minority of a little over five million having power over a total population of thirty-six million blacks, "coloreds," Indians, and others.

Apartheid in action, March 1990. Armed South African police battle with a trade union member taking part in a peaceful march through Pretoria. Under the state of emergency then in force, riot police dispersed the marchers using clubs and dogs.

Apartheid was not invented in 1948. The notion of racial segregation has a long history in South Africa, dating back almost three hundred years. In this book we look at the history of segregation and at the reasons why the system of apartheid came to an end. We examine the conditions that kept the white minority in power for so long and we anticipate the likely consequences of the end of apartheid.

One of the questions that has divided historians and commentators on South African affairs is whether white people had the right to claim land in southern Africa. Defenders of apartheid have argued that there were very few inhabitants when the Dutch first settled there in 1652. What is clear is that to understand apartheid we must look back several hundred years to when Europeans first set foot on southern African soil.

A STRATEGIC COLONY

White men first established a toehold in South Africa when they realized its importance as a midpoint on the trade route between Europe and the East Indies. The Portuguese were the first Europeans to explore the region as early as the fifteenth century. Other Europeans followed, including the English and the Dutch. The sixteenth to the nineteenth centuries were a

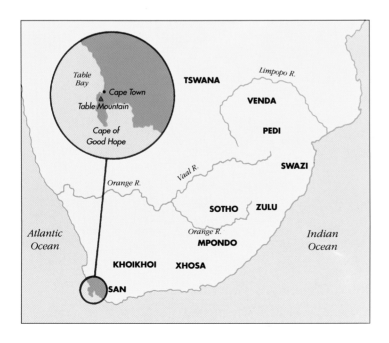

This map shows the different peoples living in southern Africa at the time Jan van Riebeeck established his fort on land that is today part of Cape Town. The Khoikhoi and San, the native peoples of the tip of southern Africa, were forced to give up their land and become slaves or move north. Over generations other black peoples drifted from the north into southern Africa along the narrow coastal belt and through the central plateau.

7

The war, British chiefs, is an unjust one; for you are striving to extirpate a people whom you forced to take up arms. When our fathers, and the fathers of the Boers, first settled the Suurveld, they dwelt together in peace, until the herds of the Amaxhosa [Xhosa] increased so as to make the hearts of the Boers sore. What these covetous men could not get from our fathers for old buttons, they took by force. Our fathers drove them [the Boers] out of the Suurveld. The white men hated us, but could not drive us away. You came at last like locusts. We stood: we could do no more.

A speech on behalf of a Xhosa war-prophet called Makanda in 1819, from Thomas Pringle's Narrative of a Residence in South Africa.

period of colonial expansion, during which the European powers conquered land in order to increase their access to spices, sugar, and other products to trade.

The Dutch decided they needed a base at the Cape of Good Hope (the southernmost tip of South Africa) to supply ships sailing between Europe and the Far East. In 1652 the Dutch East India Company sent a group of merchants to build a fort there. This would enable ships "to refresh themselves with vegetables, meat, water and other necessities by which means the sick on board [might] be restored to health." Jan van Riebeeck, the merchants' leader, soon discovered that the kitchen gardens planted to supply his people were costly to run and inadequate. In 1657 he persuaded the Dutch East India Company to allow nine company employees to set themselves up as farmers. They were given plots of land near Table Bay, so that they could supply vegetables, fruit, grain, and meat to the company. These nine men were the first Afrikaners, or Boers (the word "boer" is Dutch for farmer).

So who were the native peoples of southern Africa in 1652? The natives of the Cape were two tribes of closely related people called the Khoikhoi and the San, both had light brown skin and were small in height. The Khoikhoi numbered around 100,000 and the San around 20,000. The San were nomadic hunters who kept no livestock, but the Khoikhoi were herders who possessed a valuable commodity in the eyes of the Dutch – meat. Initially the Dutch bought meat from the Khoikhoi, but the situation changed after the 1657

This 1676 engraving shows Dutch settlers at Cape Town overseeing the arrival of slaves. Some early white settlers married slaves, but many had children by slaves out of wedlock. In 1671 the Dutch East India Company's commissioner at the Cape noted that three-quarters of the children born to company slave-women had European fathers.

granting of lands to Dutch East India Company workers. There began a conflict between Afrikaner and native, as the white farmers increasingly took over the grazing lands of the Khoikhoi. Although Jan van Riebeeck planted a hedge to keep the Khoikhoi out, it was the white settlers themselves who soon moved beyond this boundary.

Van Riebeeck had used Khoikhoi labor to build his fort and maintain his ships; but as the level of work rapidly increased he saw the need for a sturdier and more controllable workforce. He asked the Dutch East India Company to supply him with slaves. The company agreed, and a few shiploads of slaves were sent in from Madagascar, Angola, and Dahomey and later from Zanzibar and Mozambique. Domestic slaves were imported from India, Ceylon, and Indonesia to undertake household duties. Four distinct categories of citizenship were recognized by the Dutch authorities: company employees, free citizens (Boers), slaves, and native people. White people were regarded as superior and were granted more rights.

In the centuries that followed, the South African natives suffered immeasurably from the effects of white settlers. The Khoikhoi, having been dispossessed of their lands, died as a result of diseases introduced by Europeans, most devastatingly the smallpox epidemic of 1713. In the nineteenth century the San were systematically exterminated by Boer hunting parties; the few survivors were forced to move north. As Boer settlers also moved north and eastward from the Cape they came into conflict with dark-brown-skinned South African peoples. These were the Xhosa, Zulu, and other Bantu speakers, and the Sotho and Tswana peoples, themselves migrating southward.

A Zulu warrior, photographed in 1897. Throughout the nineteenth century the Zulu Army, with its reputation for courage, discipline, and ruthlessness, successfully countered both British and Boer forces. In 1887 the Zulus were finally defeated by imperial troops determined to gain control of South Africa's mineral wealth.

BRITISH RULE

In 1836-37 groups of Boers (Afri-kaners) left their homes at the Cape and pressed inland across the Drakensberg Mountains. Within nine years, some 14,000 had settled land in the interior. To the Afrikaners, their "Great Trek" is a sacred saga on a par with the Biblical Exodus when God brought the Israelites, his chosen people, to the promised land.

The nineteenth century saw the colonization of southern Africa by the British and the military defeat of the Xhosa, Zulus, and other peoples of the interior. The warlike reputation of the Zulus derived from the great warrior Shaka, who reorganized the Zulu Army into an efficient fighting unit and embarked on a series of wars against neighboring peoples in the early 1800s. The Zulu Army, fighting with spears and shields, inflicted a major defeat on British troops, armed with artillery and guns at Isandlwhana on January 22, 1879. It was eight years – from 1879 to 1887 – before the British Army defeated the Zulus and Zululand finally became a British colony.

By the nineteenth century the notion of white master and black slave had become an acceptable part of white South African life. For the Boers, the original

peasant farmers, slave ownership was considered to be a God-given right. But the extension of the British Empire in southern Africa led to conflict between the British and the Boers. After 1815, the best commercial opportunities in Cape Town required fluency in English, which also became the language used in the law courts, by the administration, and in education; and in 1834 slavery was abolished throughout the British Empire. During 1836 and 1837 some 6,000 Boers expressed their anger with the British way of running affairs at the Cape by embarking on "The Great Trek." They loaded their families and belongings onto wagons and set out for Natal, which was then quickly annexed by the British. The Boers pressed farther inland and set up the Boer republics known as the Orange Free State and Transvaal. But Boer independence was to be short-lived. The discovery of diamonds at Kimberley in 1871 and of gold in the Transvaal in 1886 concentrated British efforts on gaining control of these areas. The essentially agricultural interior was rapidly transformed into a more urban economy, requiring money and cheap labor to take advantage of the mineral wealth.

As British companies assumed control of the mines, they employed black men as miners, brick-makers, water-carriers, and traders. The miners came from all over southern Africa. They left their families for as long as the work lasted and were housed in men-only compounds (unlike their white counterparts, who had better paid jobs and were allowed to bring their wives and live in town). Thus started the migrant labor system which was later to become one of the main pillars of apartheid. The mine owners took little responsibility for the men housed in the compounds. If they fell ill, these employees were sent home to their people who (it was assumed) would care for them for free.

In 1877 the British annexation of Transvaal eventually led to the first Anglo-Boer War in 1880–81, after which the British were forced to withdraw from the Transvaal. The discovery of gold at the heart of the Boer republics led to further tension and, in 1899, the second Anglo-Boer War broke out. The war was over by 1902, with the Boers defeated, but it left a legacy of resentment and anti-British feeling. The Boer generals won the political victory when in 1910 the British gave the four South African colonies of Transvaal, the Orange Free State, Natal, and the Cape self-rule as the Union of South Africa. This effort to create goodwill essentially split control of South Africa between the Afrikaners and the British, at the expense of the black population who were left with few rights.

The country's new leaders were responsible for instituting many of the new apartheid laws. The most

Boer fighters capture a British convoy during the second Anglo-Boer War in 1900. The Boers fought a guerrilla war and inflicted heavy losses on the British, who set up prison compounds (the forerunners of Nazi concentration camps) for Boer women and children. The primitive conditions in these camps meant that some 16,168 died from wounds and disease.

The last hundred years have witnessed a miracle behind which must lie a divine plan. Indeed, the history of the Afrikaner reveals a will and determination which makes one feel that Afrikanerdom is not the work of men but the creation of God.

Daniel Malan, National Party prime minister, 1948.

The discovery of diamonds in the 1870s attracted Europeans desperate to make their fortunes. They included Cecil John Rhodes, who became one of South Africa's richest men and prime minister of the Cape.

hated measure was the Native Land Act of 1913 which allocated 92.7 percent of the land to a total of one-and-a-half million whites and left the remaining 7.3 percent for five-and-a-half-million blacks. (In 1936 the South African Native Trust bought more land, making a total of 11.7 percent for the black population.) There were other segregation controls dating back to the nineteenth century, including the Pass Laws, under which all black men had to carry documents showing they had permission to be in town and that they had paid their taxes up to date. There was a somewhat more liberal tradition at the Cape which gave black people and coloreds (the descendants of the Khoikhoi, of mixed marriages, and of slaves and freemen brought in from Indonesia), who made up 15 percent of the population there, voting rights but did not allow them to have representatives in parliament. (Voting rights for blacks and coloreds at the Cape were, however, removed by the Nationalist government in the 1950s.)

The segregation measures were no harsher than those of many other colonized countries at that time. What was different in South Africa was that segregation in the form of apartheid continued long after the colonial system had been dismantled in other countries, and that the whites had no intention of handing over power to the black majority.

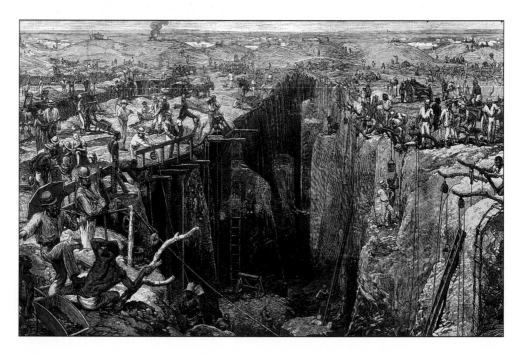

AN APARTHEID STATE

In 1948, in a poll confined to two million whites and a few "colored" voters, the National Party of South Africa was elected by a narrow majority. The National Party was the party of Afrikaner nationalism, a spirit that had been fostered since the defeat of the two Afrikaner republics in the second Anglo-Boer War. "Today South Africa belongs to us once more," gloated leader Daniel Malan upon his coming into power. Building on the existing segregationist system, and thus ignoring the voices of eight million South African black people who had not been allowed to vote, the Nationalists set about producing laws to create apartheid.

In many ways, the setting up of apartheid was simply the legalization of an already well-established system. What was different about South Africa was that it was now out of step with the rest of the world. At this point in history, segregation was being outlawed in the United States and colonial forms of government were breaking down throughout Africa and Asia, as the empires of Great Britain, France, and other European countries crumbled. One of the by-products of World War II (1939–45) was the idea, established in the Atlantic Charter, that people should be allowed to govern themselves. Within South Africa that would have given all South Africans the right to vote, and would therefore have meant an end to white rule.

The main steps to apartheid were taken in a series of laws passed in a relatively short period of time. The Prohibition of Mixed Marriages

Dr. Daniel Malan, an ex-clergyman with the Dutch Reformed Church, was eighty years old when he became prime minister. His policies were guided by a belief in the supremacy of the Afrikaner people, a goal he attained by limiting civil rights for others.

Racial relations cannot improve if the wrong type of education is given to the Natives. They cannot improve if the result of Native education is the creation of frustrated people who, as a result of the education they received, have expectations in life which circumstances in South Africa do not allow to be fulfilled immediately.

Hendrik Verwoerd in 1953.

Dr. Hendrik Verwoerd, the influential apartheid propagandist, became prime minister in 1958. In 1966 he was knifed and killed by a mentally disturbed man as he sat in the Assembly, but even after his death his theories on apartheid provided the framework for government policies.

Act 1949 outlawed marriages between the races. An amendment to the Immorality Act in 1950 banned sexual relations between whites and any other race group. The Population Registration Act 1950 created a legal definition of race and classified everybody into one of four races: white, native (later changed to Bantu), colored, and Indian. (Bantu is the name given to a group of languages spoken by almost all people living in southern Africa, but the word came to be used by the South African state as a disrespectful, racist term for black African people generally.) The Group Areas Act of 1950 allowed the government to create totally separate living and working areas. It also prevented people of one race group owning property in an area reserved for another.

The Pass Law that the British had introduced in the nineteenth century to regulate the movement of nonwhites in South Africa was tightened up by the Natives Abolition of Passes Act in 1952. This subjected black people to punishment if they did not have a document called a reference book. By introducing the reference book the Nationalists claimed to have abolished passes, but in effect the new system was much stricter, as the book had to be carried at all times and presented to the police on demand. The Separate Amenities Act 1953 tried to separate the races completely by removing coloreds, Indians, and natives to the outskirts of urban areas. It also instituted the separation of public facilities such as trains, buses, beaches, and park benches.

In 1953 the Bantu Education Act took control of African education from state-aided mission schools and handed it over to the Department of Native Affairs, a government unit headed by the energetic Dr. Hendrik Verwoerd. "Bantu education" was one of the most hated aspects of the apartheid regime. It decreed a separate (and inferior) education for black children, which meant that they would never be able to compete with whites in the labor market. The Act of 1953 restricted the powers of church schools where liberal tradition had ensured that black children received at least a limited amount of quality education.

In 1958 Hendrik Verwoerd became prime minister. Verwoerd had been in many ways the "architect" of apartheid and its chief supporter, so it is instructive to look at the basis of his beliefs. He was born in the Netherlands and came to South Africa at the age of two. He lived in an English suburb of Cape Town for a while before moving to Rhodesia. As a non-Afrikaner, he had a strong need to identify himself as one and so became an enthusiastic Afrikaner nationalist. He studied religious theories and went to Germany in the 1930s where he saw Adolf Hitler's racist policies at firsthand. Verwoerd identified with Nazi philosophy, a feature of which was to see the Germans as the master race and all others, for example, Jewish people, gypsies, and Slavs as inferior. Many Afrikaners had enormous sympathy for the Germans during World War II – much of it inspired by traditional hatred of the British.

THE HOMELANDS

In 1961 Verwoerd's government decided on the policy of "bantustans" or "homelands." Native reserves, or

A map showing the patchwork effect of setting up the ten bantustans or "homelands" in 1961. Only four homelands accepted "independence" offered by the South African government in the 1970s and 1980s, they were Ciskei, Bophuthatswana, Transkei, and Venda.

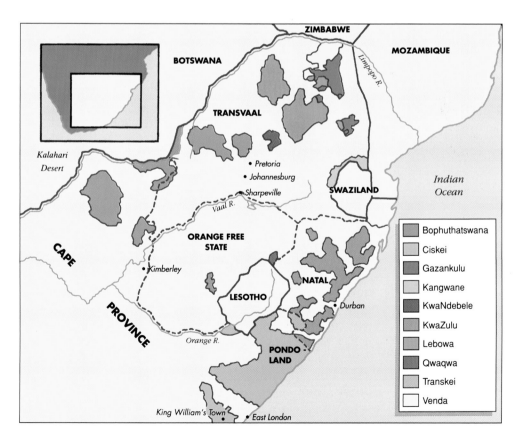

A resettlement village in the KwaZulu homeland, Natal, showing that even by 1982 life had not improved for the people living there. Hundreds of thousands of people were forcibly removed to such villages from 1948 onward.

When this Bill [Bantu Education Act] becomes law, it will not be the parents but the Department of Native Affairs which will decide whether an African child should receive higher or other education. It might well be that the children of those who fight the Government and its policies will almost certainly be taught how to drill rocks in mines and how to plough potatoes on the farms of Bethal.

Nelson Mandela, ANC leader, in 1953.

"homelands," had been constituted under the 1913 Native Land Act. Eventually they amounted to 13 percent of the land in South Africa and were the only areas in which black people could acquire land legally. The idea of the mass of the country being designated "white" with smaller black homelands came from the traditional Afrikaner notion of baaskap or "mastery" – white domination that was practiced by the earliest Dutch settlers and their descendants. The constitution of the South African Republic (Transvaal) stated: "There shall be no equality in State or Church between white and black." Both the Dutch and British colonial governments had tried to keep whites and blacks apart with little success: the problem was how to police the border between them. By the 1940s and 1950s many whites in South Africa were afraid of being "swamped" by the blacks and clung to a belief in their innate superiority.

Verwoerd's government recognized ten homelands, belonging to ten different "ethnic nationalities," who were given the right to self-determination in their "traditional areas." Verwoerd admitted that this was a response to international pressure on South Africa: "a form of fragmentation which we would not have liked if we were able to avoid it thereby buying the white man his freedom and right to retain domination in what is his country." This seemingly moderate move was a way of appearing to give some political rights to the black population. In reality it split the black people into "independent" states too small and weak ever to challenge white rule.

Verwoerd's vision of South Africa saw the blacks

living completely separate lives in their homelands. Using phrases such as "separate development" and "separate freedoms," Verwoerd believed that by 1978 the millions of blacks living in "white" South Africa would go to live in their own homelands, attracted by the prospect of full rights and their own nationhood. Then the black townships, the settlements that had sprung up outside "white cities," would no longer be needed. Some migrant workers from the homelands would be allowed to work in "white" South Africa but they would merely be "guest workers," who would return to their separate nations once their work was done.

A basic disadvantage of the homelands was that it was impossible for the people living there to become self-sufficient. The land was mostly scrub or rock-filled, of such poor quality that it could never have produced enough to feed all the people, had they remained. In order to support their families black men, and some women, sought work in the more prosperous areas of South Africa – those areas designated for whites. Up to the 1980s over 70 percent of the economically active population in the homelands was dependent on the migrant labor system. Thus developed one of apartheid's most distinctive features: while black men worked as "aliens" (with no workers' rights) in the white cities, older people, women, and children barely survived in the rural squalor of the homelands. During the first decades of apartheid, the white government provided economic stability, and foreign money flowed in ($3.6 billion in 1960, rising to $7.9 bil-

If the native in South Africa today in any kind of school in existence is being taught to expect that he will live his adult life under a policy of equal rights, he is making a big mistake. There is no place for him in the European community above the level of certain forms of labour.

Hendrik Verwoerd, National Party prime minister 1958–66.

Migrant workers from a gold mine near Johannesburg eat a meal in their compound living quarters. The mine owners employed men from the homelands as well as from neighboring countries such as Lesotho, Mozambique, Botswana, and Swaziland.

17

lion in 1970). South Africa therefore experienced an unexpected economic boom which served to foster the illusion that apartheid could work.

Enforcing the policy of separate development involved the massive forced removal of the population. Between 1960 and 1983 more than three-and-a-half million people were moved from "white" South Africa into the homelands, or from one homeland to another. Some industrialists set up factories in the homelands where they were able to pay very low wages, but the trend towards the urbanization of black people was irreversible and the black urban population grew in spite of apartheid. In 1951 there were one-and-a-half million black city dwellers; by 1980 their number had swollen to more than seven-and-a-quarter million. As an illustration of the whites' eagerness to relocate the black population we need only look at what happened in Sophiatown. Between 1955 and 1960 this black town less than four miles to the west of Johannesburg was cleared of its people, demolished, and replaced by Triomph, a white suburb. Most of the people from Sophiatown went to Soweto, a township on the outskirts of Johannesburg.

THE TOWNSHIPS

Although South Africa's industrial development depended on cheap black labor, the National Party had ideological reasons for wanting blacks to live in the homelands. As Verwoerd put it: "If South Africa has to

The black township of Soweto was built in 1954 to accommodate the 60,000 inhabitants of Sophiatown. As increasing numbers of black people migrated to the cities, Soweto became home to more than two million. Severe health problems were caused by overcrowding, and many houses had no sewage facilities.

Squatter camps, such as this one near Cape Town, grew up because no new housing for black people was built in the cities. A cycle of existence developed in the camps, as people built shacks which were then bull-dozed by govern- ment employees. The inhabitants would return later to rebuild their makeshift homes.

choose between being poor and white or rich and mul-tiracial, then it must choose to be white." Meanwhile World War II had seen a rapid expansion in South Africa's manufacturing capabilities. Local demand for goods had increased because imports from Europe had ceased during the war. There was also demand from the Allies for arms, ammunition, and ship repairs. By 1943 manufacturing had become more important than mining in terms of production and providing work, and Afrikaners moved into the commercial and industrial job vacancies created by the departure of English-speaking whites to fight in the war. As a result, there was a movement of black people into skilled and semi-skilled jobs from which they had been barred.

As far back as 1923, the Natives (Urban Areas) Act had required urban local authorities to provide segre-gated "locations" or townships for nonwhite guest workers. The townships consisted of basic housing which blacks with work permits were allowed to rent; but they still had no security of tenure and could be removed from their homes without warning. South Africa's largest township sprang up southwest of Johannesburg and became known as the South-Western Township or Soweto. From the 1950s the townships were internally divided along "ethnic" lines and separated from towns inhabited by other "racial" groups (generally whites) by industrial areas or buffer strips. Workers were transported to and from these townships daily, often rising before dawn and return-ing home very late. The exodus of blacks from the homelands into the urban areas resulted in the growth

All the Bantu have their permanent homes in the Reserves and their entry into other areas and into the urban areas is mere-ly of a temporary nature and for eco-nomic reasons. In other words, they are admitted as work-seekers, not as settlers.

Dr. W. W. M. Eiselen, Afrikaner ideologist, in 1952.

THE END OF APARTHEID

of squatter camps near Johannesburg and other large cities, as people looking for jobs built temporary homes for themselves in and around the townships.

On a personal level apartheid produced much human suffering. Families were divided by race classification: brothers were not allowed to travel on the same bus to school because they had different skin color; white parents ran the risk of having their children classified as colored and forbidden to live with them. In 1966 some 479,114 blacks were prosecuted for offenses under the Pass Laws. In 1967 some 511 people were convicted under the Immorality Act for having sexual relations with those of a different race.

Perhaps the single positive achievement of the 1948 election was that it finally pushed the black population into a form of active resistance. As Chief Albert Luthuli, African National Congress president from 1952-67, said: "I doubt whether many of us realized at the time that the very intensity of Nationalist oppression would do what we had so far failed to achieve – awake the mass of Africans to political awareness, goad us finally out of resigned endurance." It was this political awakening that was to sound the death knell of apartheid.

The single distinguishing feature of this everyday scene is a government notice declaring the beach a "whites only" area. This open racism, set out in the 1953 Separate Amenities Act, made the South African system difficult to justify to the rest of the world. The act was abolished in 1990.

BLACK RESISTANCE

A major cause of the end of apartheid was that black resistance made South Africa ungovernable. In this chapter we shall look at what lay behind the black peoples' response to the apartheid state.

The main organization to challenge white South Africa's policies was the African National Congress (ANC), which was originally founded in 1912. The ANC's aims were to act as a pressure group for democratic change and against racial laws. Its leaders believed that South Africa belonged to all who lived there regardless of race, and they aimed to use "passive action or continued movement" to achieve their objectives. Originally the ANC was formed to pro-

A passive resistance march in Johannesburg in 1952. The government responded to peaceful actions such as this by sending in the police, who arrested demonstrators and imprisoned the leaders.

mote the interests of the black professional middle-class, but by 1920 it was extending its support to striking miners. It did not start to build a mass membership until 1940, and even then did not take an active part in mass protests such as bus boycotts and the squatter movement. However in the 1940s, under the leadership of Dr. A. B. Xuma, it issued its first political program calling for "one man, one vote," abolition of the Pass Laws, trade union rights, better health facilities, and education for black people. The Congress Youth League was formed in 1943 with a radical Program of Action demanding strikes, boycotts, and civil disobedience. It recruited energetic people like Nelson Mandela, Oliver Tambo, and Walter Sisulu, and its more militant Program was adopted by the ANC in 1949.

Following the National Party victory in 1948 and the introduction of the first apartheid laws, the government passed the Suppression of Communism Act 1950. This act allowed the government to suppress any form of dissent within a very broad definition of

Another early protest against apartheid involved burning or throwing away the hated pass books. These documents contained personal details and had to be presented to the police on demand. By law, every black person over the age of sixteen was obliged to carry a pass book or risk immediate arrest.

During the 1940s and 1950s the ANC formed close links with radical Indians and coloreds. Here colored sympathizers shake hands with Nelson Mandela, arrested for his part in the Defiance Campaign. The nonviolent action of the 1952 campaign was inspired by Mahatma Gandhi, spiritual leader of India.

communism, and it was used against the ANC. The first group to be banned under the act was the South African Communist Party (SACP), which went underground and reformed secretly to continue its work, though many of its members joined the ANC instead. In 1952 the ANC launched the Defiance Campaign, its first mass action. This involved confrontation through passive resistance and challenging petty apartheid restrictions like using "white" entrances in shops. It encouraged people to throw their passes away, which would lead to their arrest, causing the state considerable expense and inconvenience. Within a few months, more than 8,500 people had been arrested. As leaders were detained or banned under the Suppression of Communism Act, the campaign ground to a halt. Nonetheless, ANC membership had been increased to around 100,000.

In 1952 the ANC elected Albert Luthuli, a former teacher and chief of a small Zulu clan, as its president (Mr. Luthuli was awarded the Nobel Peace Prize in 1961). Around the same time, the Congress Alliance was formed to coordinate policies among the ANC, the Indian Congress, the recently formed Colored People's Organization, the nonracial South African Congress of Trade Unions (SACTU), and the Congress of Democrats (a white group). At the Congress of the People held at Kliptown near Johannesburg on June 25-26, 1955, a Freedom Charter was drawn up, proposing a nonracial South

The people shall govern!
All national groups shall have equal rights!
The people shall share in the country's wealth!
The land shall be shared among those who work it!
All shall be equal before the law!

From the ANC Freedom Charter, 1955.

Africa with equal rights and justice for all. The charter drew on socialist ideals and demanded a redistribution of wealth in South Africa. The movement against apartheid was still searching for nonviolent, political strategies with which to fight the government. The government response, however, was to arrest 156 of the congress delegates and put them on trial for treason.

THE SHARPEVILLE MASSACRE

Not everyone in the ANC was happy with the Freedom Charter. The Africanists, led by Robert Sobukwe, felt that black nationalists should fight the government to win South Africa for black people – not join forces with "Communist-inspired whites." In April 1959 Sobukwe and his followers left the ANC to form the Pan-Africanist Congress (PAC). As the ANC was planning a massive anti-pass campaign to take place in March 1960, the PAC tried to forestall it by announcing its own anti-pass day. On March 21, 1960, the PAC succeeded in assembling a crowd of around

Who will deny that thirty years of my life have been spent knocking in vain, patiently, moderately and modestly at a closed and barred door? What have been the fruits of moderation? The past thirty years have seen the greatest number of laws restricting our rights and progress, until today we have reached a stage where we have almost no rights at all.

Chief Albert Luthuli, president-general of the ANC in the 1950s.

Chief Albert Luthuli speaking at Oslo University where he was awarded the 1961 Nobel Peace Prize. An advocate of nonviolent action, Luthuli was one of the ANC's most popular and courageous leaders.

5,000 supporters outside the police station at Sharpeville in the Transvaal. A scuffle broke out near one of the gates to the police compound, and a police officer was knocked over. As the crowd surged forward to see what was happening, the police opened fire. The crowd turned and fled. The dead numbered 69 people, with 180 wounded; nearly all of them had been shot in the back.

The Sharpeville massacre sent shock waves throughout the world and was thoroughly condemned by many Western governments. Though moves at the United Nations to impose economic penalties on South Africa were blocked by the United States and the United Kingdom, they caused a panic among investors in South Africa, many of whom responded by removing their money. On March 30 the South African government reacted by declaring a temporary state of emergency and by arresting thousands of political activists. One week after Sharpeville, the ANC and PAC were banned under the Suppression of Communism Act. On a visit in February 1960 British prime minister Harold Macmillan had warned white South Africa of the degree of black resistance to its government's policies. In a speech to parliament in Cape Town he spoke of the "winds of change" sweeping Africa. But events in Sharpeville the following

South African police walk amid the bodies at Sharpeville on March 21, 1960. Sixty-nine people were killed when police opened fire on a crowd of demonstrators.

During my lifetime I have dedicated my life to this struggle of the African people. I have fought against white domination, and I have fought against black domination. I have cherished the ideal of a democratic and free society in which all persons live together in harmony with equal opportunities. It is an ideal which I hope to live for, and to see realized. But my lord, if needs be, it is an ideal for which I am prepared to die.

Nelson Mandela, ANC leader, at his trial in 1964.

Blacks are suffering from an inferiority complex – a result of 300 years of deliberate oppression, denigration and derision.

Steve Biko, Black Consciousness leader, 1968–77.

month demonstrated how wide the ideological gulf had become between South Africa and other Commonwealth nations. In 1961 Verwoerd took South Africa out of the Commonwealth (the organization of former colonies of the British Empire), and embarked on a policy of refraining from foreign economic and political relations.

The banning of the ANC and PAC forced both to go underground. The ANC sent Oliver Tambo to Bechuanaland (later to become Botswana) to lead the struggle from exile. It also set up a military wing, known as Umkhonto we Sizwe (Spear of the Nation) under Nelson Mandela although he, like other ANC leaders, had neither military nor underground experience. In December 1961 Umkhonto launched a two-year sabotage campaign aimed at the destruction of property, by exploding its first homemade bombs. But by 1964 the Umkhonto leaders, including Mandela and Walter Sisulu, had been captured and sentenced to life imprisonment. The PAC, which had also set up a military wing less organized and more violent than Umkhonto, was infiltrated by police informers and almost 3,000 members were arrested simultaneously. Black resistance was thus effectively stifled during the late 1960s and early 1970s.

Although the government could ban leaders and arrest troublemakers, it could not prevent young blacks feeling resentful about the poor education they received and the general lack of opportunities offered to them. In 1968 a young medical student called Stephen Biko was involved in setting up an all-black South African students' organization. Biko was a student at Natal University's nonwhite medical school, and he was to seize a moment that the government had not foreseen when they created separate universities for blacks and whites. By placing young black intellectuals in their own "tribal colleges," the government had unwittingly provided ideal conditions for the nurturing of "Black Consciousness." Inspired by the Black Power movement in the United States, the main theme of Black Consciousness was that black people should develop a positive consciousness about being black, then they would feel empowered to undertake the political action which would gain them their freedom. The movement was highly influential in South Africa during the late 1960s and 1970s, where it specified the exclusion of whites but included African, Indian, and "so-called colored" within the term "black."

THE SOWETO UPRISING

The next phase of black resistance to apartheid originated with the children of the Soweto township.
Angry about the forced use of Afrikaans in their
schools, the children of Soweto planned a mass
protest on June 16, 1976. Some 10,000 children were
assembled outside a secondary school, when the police
arrived and started firing tear gas into the crowd. The
children responded by throwing stones at the police
who opened fire, killing at least one child. The Soweto
incident inflamed the black people of the townships
and days of rioting followed. On June 26 the government dropped the ruling about Afrikaans being
taught in schools. The children had won. Many young
black people left South Africa after the Soweto uprising to join Umkhonto units in Zambia and Tanzania.
The death of Steve Biko in suspicious circumstances
while in police custody in September 1977, and the
banning of Black Consciousness groups the following
month, left a political vacuum in South Africa. In May
1978 a new Black Consciousness movement emerged
called the Azanian People's Organization (AZAPO)
and directed toward the black working class.

*Riot police move
in on demonstra-
tors in Cape Town
during the 1976
uprising.*

In 1983 South Africa's prime minister P. W. Botha announced the introduction of a new constitution. Aware that, while blacks had homelands in which they could exercise their rights (however limited), coloreds and Indians had no rights whatsoever, Botha gave whites, coloreds, and Indians each a House, or legislative assembly, in a three part parliament. The proportion of whites to nonwhites, however, would always ensure white domination. The colored and Indian parliaments had no voice in foreign affairs, few Indians or coloreds stood for office, and not many of them voted.

If Botha's expensive parliamentary reforms did not work, neither did the government's plan for blacks to elect local authorities in the townships. In August 1983 the United Democratic Front (UDF) was launched to coordinate resistance to the new constitution. The UDF was made up of student, youth, women's, and

In King William's Town, Transkei, pallbearers carry the casket of Black Consciousness leader Steve Biko through a huge crowd of mourners at his funeral on September 25, 1977. Biko died of critical injuries sustained to the head while in police custody.

President P. W. Botha, whose commitment to a new constitution did not extend to black majority rule. His unsuccessful attempts to reform apartheid resulted in a nationwide state of emergency being called in 1986.

other antiapartheid groups, and one of its most prominent campaigners was Dr. Allan Boesak. Botha's new constitution did not produce the intended results: international acceptance and the support of the non-white middle classes. Instead it coincided with the start of the most violent period of South Africa's history. The UDF had led a successful boycott of the 1984 council elections in black townships; very few blacks had bothered, or dared, to vote. The new councillors were mostly middle-class blacks who were optimistic about the possibilities for cooperation between black people and the white government. But they underestimated the anger of the township people.

The violence started in Sharpeville, where the newly elected deputy mayor was hacked to death. The unrest then spread throughout South Africa. It lasted for three years, from 1984 to 1986, and led to more than 3,000 deaths, 30,000 detentions, and great damage to property as well as to South Africa's image abroad. Blacks now directed their anger toward fellow blacks they believed to be collaborators with the white

We conceive of our country as a single, united, democratic and non-racial state, belonging to all who live in it, in which all shall enjoy equal rights, and in which sovereignty will come from the people as a whole, and not from a collection of Bantustans and racial tribal groups organized to perpetuate minority power.

Oliver Tambo, ANC leader.

authorities. An ugly side to the uprising was the practice of "necklacing," a word used to describe the killing of a person by placing a gasoline filled tire around their neck and setting it alight.

The uprising did not succeed in making South Africa ungovernable, but it did succeed in splitting the South African government between those in favor of making concessions and reforms and those against. South Africa could now only be ruled by imposing states of emergency, involving tight control of media coverage and political repression on an unprecedented scale. The imprisonment of black leaders, successful in the 1950s and 1960s, no longer worked. Order could only be restored by using the army to take over the townships. Although the violence was mostly over by 1986, black people continued to resist by boycotting elections and shops and by striking. The 1984–86 uprising brought about a financial crisis, as South Africa had greater difficulty in attracting foreign investment money and the value of its own money collapsed. It became clear that government repression could not continue indefinitely. The scene was set for the destruction of apartheid.

A car blazes during riots in Duduza township, west of Johannesburg, in 1984. Throughout the 1980s there was a growing prevalence of black-on-black violence in the townships.

SANCTIONS AND EXTERNAL PRESSURE

South Africa is a country rich in minerals. It is the world's main producer of gold, chromite, and platinum and also has rich deposits of coal, copper, iron ore, manganese, silver, uranium, antimony phosphate, vanadium, and diamonds. But it does not have any oil and has to import heavy machinery for its factories, as well as electronic equipment and trucks. South Africa is therefore dependent on international trade to sell its minerals and buy oil. Although only a third of its farmland receives enough rain to grow crops easily, it produces apples, grapes (and therefore wine), corn,

Sustained international pressure and economic sanctions played a very important role in ensuring that it became impossible to continue with apartheid.

Nelson Mandela, ANC leader, 1994.

Bishop Desmond Tutu was an outspoken critic of apartheid, often interviewed by Western media. Church leaders tended to gain prominence in the fight against apartheid, because political leaders were banned and imprisoned, and Tutu was regarded by many as the voice of moderation. In the 1980s he became archbishop of Cape Town and in 1984 was awarded the Nobel Peace Prize.

When the ladder is falling, surely it's those at the top who will get hurt most, not those at the bottom?

Archbishop Desmond Tutu, general secretary of the South African Council of Churches.

President Ronald Reagan and Prime Minister Margaret Thatcher meet for talks in London in 1985. As opponents of sanctions, they both believed the South African government's claim that black nationalists were "revolutionaries" and that reforms of apartheid would somehow lead to a peaceful solution.

oranges, pineapples, potatoes, sugarcane, tobacco, and wheat, some of which it exports. Its major trading partners are the United Kingdom, Germany, France, the United States, and Japan and many of these countries invest directly in South Africa. As the most industrialized country in southern Africa it dominates the region, recruiting cheap labor from neighboring countries to work in the mines and exporting its goods to those countries. Over the years, antiapartheid campaigners in the United States and the United Kingdom have argued that apartheid could end if Western countries were to impose sanctions on South Africa. Sanctions, or pressure, on a country can involve economic, financial and trade boycotts, corporate withdrawals, and disinvestment. ("Disinvestment" is a term used to describe the action taken by a company or business when it stops trading in a country.)

Calls for sanctions go back many years. In 1959 Chief Albert Luthuli, president of the ANC, said: "The economic boycott of South Africa will entail undoubted hardship for the Africans. We do not doubt that. But if it is a method which shortens the day of bloodshed, the suffering to us will be a price we are willing to pay. In any case, we suffer already, our children are undernourished, and on a small scale (so far) we die at the whim of a policeman." Many others echoed his views, most notably in the 1980s the archbishop of Cape Town, Desmond Tutu. But a number of staunch antiapartheid activists, including member of parliament Helen Suzman, opposed economic sanctions because they feared that they would harm the blacks more than the wealthy whites.

AN ISOLATED NATION

What kind of external pressures have successive South African governments experienced over their apartheid policies? In 1946 India ended trade and diplomatic relations with South Africa and, by 1964, had cut all links with the apartheid regime. In contrast, the South African government received unspoken support from the Western world during the early years of apartheid. Following the Sharpeville massacre in 1960, the UN General Assembly made various resolutions in favor of sanctions but these were repeatedly vetoed by the United Kingdom, France, and the United States. In 1963 a voluntary arms embargo was instituted by the UN Security Council, although the United Kingdom and France did not vote. In 1973 oil exporters – members of the Organization of Petroleum Exporting Countries (OPEC) – agreed to stop selling fuel to South Africa, and in 1974 South Africa stopped taking part in the UN General Assembly. But it took the deaths in the Soweto uprising of 1976 to get the sanctions bandwagon really rolling.

In 1977 the United Nations Security Council agreed to ban the sale of military equipment to South Africa. This created problems for the South African government, but it managed to sidestep the ban by importing through third countries, forging links with Israel and Chile which were willing to provide military support, and by building its own weapons. The main impact of these sanctions was that South Africa was unable to buy spares for its existing equipment and could not obtain up-to-date hardware. Also in 1977 the Commonwealth declared a ban on sporting contacts with South Africa and many countries decided to sever cultural links as well. This increased South Africa's sense of isolation. By the mid-1970s the oil embargo was beginning to have serious consequences on the South African economy. In 1986 President P. W. Botha admitted that it had cost the country $25 billion.

In the early 1980s the momentum of sanctions was stalled by Margaret Thatcher, prime minister of the United Kingdom, and Ronald Reagan, President of the United States. The reluctance of both these world leaders to support sanctions was rooted in their fear of a Communist-backed ANC government coming to

An antiapartheid protestor outside a branch of Barclays Bank in London urges the withdrawal of British investment in South Africa. Pressure from consumers in Western countries and loss of confidence finally led Barclays to withdraw from its South African interests.

There is no case in history that I know of where punitive, general economic sanctions have been effective to bring about internal changes.

Margaret Thatcher, United Kingdom prime minister, 1986.

Sanctions will help to convince white South Africans that it is in their own interests to dismantle apartheid and enter negotiations to establish a non-racial and representative government. The minority must see that apartheid is no longer a viable option because the economic and political cost is too high. By reducing the power and will of the apartheid state and its beneficiaries to resist change, sanctions will support and shorten the struggle.

Commonwealth Independent Expert Study on Sanctions, 1989.

Breaking the Afrikaner will by a combination of rising revolutionary violence at home and rising [economic] pressure abroad won't work. Government, like its supporting constituency, perceives black rule as a mortal threat – to language, to property, to identity, and to physical security – and it is vain to think that such fears can be overcome by mere threats to property.

The Johannesburg Business Day newspaper, 1986.

power in South Africa. They both argued that sanctions were ineffective in bringing an end to apartheid, that U.S. and UK business interests were of primary importance, that jobs at home would be lost, and that black people would suffer most as a result. Their statements came at a time when the South African government was exercising increased repression at home and making military raids into Angola, Mozambique, and elsewhere in southern Africa. As television viewers in Europe and the United States saw evidence of the increasing township violence in South Africa, there were renewed calls for sanctions. In 1984 and 1985 the United Nations agreed to press for voluntary sanctions and many European countries, including Ireland and Denmark, began to impose bans on trade with South Africa. Meanwhile Thatcher did her utmost to prevent the European Community from imposing a ban on all trade with South Africa.

The foreign action that did South Africa the most damage occurred in 1985 when Western banks refused to make any new loans and called in existing loans. South Africa was required to repay loans of $13 billion by December that year. As a result the South African currency – the rand – collapsed, losing 35 percent of its value in thirteen days. The government stopped making payments on its short-term debts and had to adjust their system of repayment, as the banks' actions meant that the country no longer had access to foreign money. External pressure intensified as U.S. and European companies pulled out of South Africa in 1986. The United Nations Economic and Social Council estimated that some 500 companies pulled out, including Coca-Cola, IBM, Metal Box, Barclays Bank, and General Motors. Furthermore Coca-Cola announced that it planned to sell its interests to black African investors. Although many of the companies sold their businesses at extremely low prices to South African employees, often Afrikaners (thus reducing the impact of their actions as the businesses continued to function), the psychological effect on South Africans was considerable. Cut off from foreign funds and unable to take part in most of the world's sporting events, with only a handful of big-name performers now prepared to visit the country, their sense of isolation further intensified.

So how effective were sanctions in bringing about the end of apartheid? The Commonwealth Independent Expert Study on Sanctions estimated that the mid-1980s sanctions cut South Africa's exports by 13 percent – a serious but not a devastating blow. In fact many African nations had to continue trading with South Africa because of its dominant economic position in the continent. However, sanctions had an impact on economic growth, which slowed down. From 1989 to 1992 South Africa experienced a serious recession, which saw its gross domestic product (GDP) go down by 3 percent every year. Although, earlier in the century, Hendrik Verwoerd had been willing to sacrifice economic growth for the sake of apartheid (see page 18), it became clear that many South African industrialists did not share his view. They needed access to foreign money and to a skilled black labor force in order to develop their businesses. If they had to decide between an apartheid state or economic prosperity, then they would choose prosperity every time.

Sanctions on the sale of arms were extremely successful and probably contributed to the military defeat suffered by the South African Defence Force at the battles of Cuito-Cuanavale in southern Angola in 1987–88 (see page 40). Many commentators see the South African withdrawal from Angola and the granting of independence to Namibia as confirmation that apartheid was in its death throes.

During the 1980s there were many organized demonstrations against apartheid in London, Washington, D.C., and other major cities, but the U.S. and UK governments were slow to respond to public opinion. Only after the 1984-86 uprising did both governments begin to exert pressure on the South African government to change.

INSTABILITY IN THE FRONTLINE STATES

The ultimate aim of the Soviet Union and its allies is to overthrow the present body politic in South Africa and to replace it with a Marxist-oriented form of government to further the objectives of the USSR.

P. W. Botha, South African prime minister 1978-89.

South African troops indiscriminately rounded up villagers, strikers and others into makeshift camps for interrogation. There was one such camp in Ondangwa, close enough to the location for us to hear the prisoners' screams. The nurses at the hospital told of soldiers bringing in bodies mangled beyond recognition, so many that the doctors in charge finally refused to accept any more. Unmarked graves appeared in the bush surrounding the camps.

An incident in 1972 described by John Ya-Otto, Namibian resistance leader, in his 1982 autobiography.

One justification for the uncertain and contradictory attitudes of Western nations toward South Africa was the argument that it was a stronghold against communism. In the years following World War II the two global superpowers, the United States and the Soviet Union, were locked in a worldwide rivalry to influence events. This rivalry became known as the Cold War, and lasted from 1945 to about 1988. During the Cold War, South Africa's position on a key Western shipping lane in the Indian Ocean and around the Cape of Good Hope was considered to be of paramount importance. Western politicians were therefore extremely anxious that a Communist regime should not seize power in South Africa.

It has been argued that the United States preferred to give unspoken support to the South African apartheid regime rather than risk the election of a Communist ANC government. But the threat of a Communist takeover in the region was probably greatly exaggerated; the advent of "Communist" regimes in Mozambique and Angola did not threaten Western interests, nor did it lead to the Soviet Union establishing bases in the region or even having much influence in those countries. However, the Soviet threat was used by the West as an excuse to give South Africa a relatively free hand in the region and to ensure the security of foreign interests there. The interests which the Western nations, particularly the United States, the United Kingdom, Germany, and Japan, had in South Africa revolved around access to South Africa's mineral wealth. To secure these interests they were anxious to maintain South Africa's internal stability, which meant suppressing black "Marxists" and maintaining the rich lifestyle of the whites.

TOWARD INDEPENDENCE

The external factor that contributed most markedly to the ending of apartheid was the Portuguese Revolution of 1974, which toppled the military dictatorship in Portugal and led to the independence of its colonies in Africa. Until 1974 South Africa had been surrounded by white-ruled colonies: Namibia (which South Africa had occupied illegally since 1949) and Angola to the west, Southern Rhodesia (now Zimbabwe) and Mozambique to the east. In 1974 the collapse of Portuguese rule in Mozambique led to the establishment of a Communist-leaning Frelimo (Front for the Liberation of Mozambique) government led by Samora Machel. In Angola the end of Portuguese domination led to a civil war with different groups fighting for power. Within five years of the end of Portuguese rule, the British white settler "government" in Southern Rhodesia was forced to negotiate a handover of power to the newly elected black government of Robert Mugabe. These nationalist victories were a great boost for the ANC and PAC, given the large numbers of young people from South Africa joining their ranks abroad. They also meant that Umkhonto

UNITA (see page 38) troops parade under a portrait of their leader, Jonas Savimbi, in Angola, 1985. UNITA was supported by the South African government; it also received military aid from the United States.

guerrillas could establish bases in these countries that were now sympathetic to their cause.

These events forced the South African government to rethink its approach to the region. In Angola there was civil war, with three parties vying for power: the Popular Movement for the Liberation of Angola (MPLA), the National Front for the Liberation of Angola (FNLA), and the National Union for the Total Independence of Angola (UNITA). All of them had at some point received help from Communist countries. MPLA forces were trained by Cuban military instructors and, in 1975, Cuba sent some 25,000 troops into Angola. The FNLA, however, had turned to the U.S. Central Intelligence Agency (CIA), which mounted a covert operation to keep the MPLA from gaining power. In secret negotiations the South African government agreed to help UNITA, and in September 1975 a task force was sent on a deep raid some 450 miles into southern Angola. It was successfully countered by MPLA forces. In northern Angola a simultaneous attack on the MPLA by FNLA forces fizzled out. With UNITA and the FNLA repulsed, South African troops had to withdraw and the MPLA was able to form a government and to occupy most of Angola's territory. The war in Angola persisted off and on until 1994, when peace was declared.

TOTAL STRATEGY

South Africa's intervention in Angola marked the beginning of a new regional policy of threatening to destabilize the governments of frontline states. This involved the intimidation of neighboring states in order that they would exclude the ANC from their territories. The South African government also extended covert military support, including the supply of arms, to organizations that opposed Communist regimes. The journalist Victoria Brittain described this policy as "the weakening, or the destruction, of a regime by an outside agency in such a way that it seems to have happened by a natural internal process." This process led to a massive militarization of South Africa, with defense spending rising from $60 million in 1960 to $3 billion in 1982. It was known, in a phrase coined by P. W. Botha, as "total strategy" – a response to the "total onslaught" that, he claimed, the world Communist conspiracy had aimed at South Africa.

We are facing an enemy bent on utter destruction. This enemy wears the mask of UNITA; but it is none other than South Africa which destroys these bridges, these trains, these villages. Their objective is that tomorrow we will give up on this difficult situation and ask South Africa for peace. But we will never give in to Pretoria's demands. With our Cuban friends and other socialist friends we can resist – and we will.

Lucio Lara, Angola's chief of party organization, in 1984.

The ANC once again affirms its support for the people of Namibia in their legitimate struggle for national independence under the leadership of SWAPO (South West Africa People's Organization). The apartheid regime must be encircled by your struggles and by your actions; by our struggle and by our actions. Together with you we shall be unconquerable and invincible.

Oliver Tambo, ANC leader.

A Mozambican soldier guards two refugees in the Tete province, 1987. It is thought that over a million people have died in the fighting in Mozambique between government forces and the South African-sponsored Renamo guerrillas.

From 1981–88, the South African Army launched operations into Angola, this time disrupting its economy. In Mozambique, South Africa supported antigovernment forces, known as Renamo. South Africa also mounted operations in Swaziland, Zimbabwe, Zambia, Lesotho, and Botswana. Because of the fighting in Angola and Mozambique, oil supplies and transportation links to the coast were disrupted. The only way that landlocked African countries could move supplies was on South African railroads. Mozambique was forced to sign a nonaggression pact with South Africa and expel its ANC representatives in Maputo. In Angola the strategy failed and UNITA lost the war; but South African involvement prolonged the fighting and Angola could not easily be used by Umkhonto to mount operations in South Africa.

We have seen that the bandits have wrecked the lives of people who could never do them any harm. They kidnapped children and abandoned them in the bush. Houses are burned down and no one can understand why they are burned down. What country do they want to govern? One without people, without houses, without roads and infrastructures? [In South Africa too] the Boers do not hesitate to kill defenseless people.

Joachim Chissano, president of Mozambique, 1987.

A major breakthrough which contributed to the end of apartheid came when South African forces were defeated by Cuban/Angolan troops in the battles of Cuito-Cuanavale in 1987–88. In July 1987 South Africa had invaded southern Angola in support of UNITA rebels. Its forces were met by the Soviet-supplied Angolan air force and antiaircraft defenses which managed to shoot down several South African aircraft. Denied air superiority, the South African Defence Force used ground troops but discovered that their ancient Centurion tanks were vulnerable to air attack. South Africa was forced to withdraw its troops and subsequently had to agree to Namibian independence in exchange for Cuban withdrawal from Angola and the removal of Umkhonto bases there.

South Africa's external policy in the frontline states of southern Africa probably helped delay the end of apartheid but it also demonstrated that it had to happen sooner or later. South Africa's military expansion was expensive and, in order to sustain it, economic growth was imperative. But economic growth depended on stability and foreign investment, both of which were undermined by the violence within South Africa. This internal violence could only be contained by military force. The South African government would have to decide whether to deploy its military might at home or abroad; it could not afford to do both.

SWAPO (South West African People's Organization) supporters celebrate their victory in the 1989 elections, in which Namibia achieved independence. South Africa had seized the country illegally in 1915. Its withdrawal from Namibia and the collapse of the apartheid regime there were an indication of things to come at home.

THE PEOPLE SHALL GOVERN!

To universal surprise South Africa's apartheid regime collapsed very rapidly. Most commentators expected the white government to hang on in a more determined manner, but having started down the road to reform those in power found they had to go the whole way and abandon apartheid completely. It was impossible to reform apartheid because it was a fundamentally flawed concept. Trying to turn back the clock by forcing the black majority to live a rural life in the homelands, where there were no jobs and few resources, could not work. The trend in South Africa, as elsewhere in the world, was for people to leave the countryside and live in the cities, where they could search for jobs. By 1993 more than 40 percent of black South Africans had relocated to urban areas.

Not all white people supported apartheid. Here women from the Black Sash civil rights organization demonstrate against apartheid laws in 1976. The Black Sash was best known for its silent "vigils" of standing women wearing black sashes in mourning at the violation of the South African constitution.

Shortly after becoming prime minister in 1958, Hendrik Verwoerd had prophesied that 1978 would be the year in which the policy of separate development would bear fruit. By this date, he declared, all the blacks would have returned to their homelands. It never happened. In 1978 Prime Minister John Vorster said that the deadline set by Verwoerd had only been a guideline, but he could not deny the fact that more and more black people were choosing to live in squatter camps adjacent to the white cities in which they worked.

The homelands never became what they were supposed to be – independent, self-supporting countries. To his credit, Mangosuthu Buthelezi, chief minister of KwaZulu and the leader of the mainly Zulu Inkatha Freedom Party, turned down the South African government's offer of "independence" for KwaZulu in the 1970s, thus blocking the progress of separate development in South Africa. KwaZulu was the fragmented homeland of South Africa's largest population group of over five million Zulus, whose territories were scattered throughout Natal. By rejecting independence (and thus clinging onto South African citizenship for his people), Buthelezi ensured that Zulus continued to outnumber whites in Natal. An aggressive opponent of apartheid, Buthelezi was convinced that a coalition government of Zulus and whites could run Natal. But ANC supporters perceived that his plan to win Natal for the Zulus was to be paid for in political terms by the black population in the rest of South Africa. As a result of Buthelezi's willingness to associate with the South African regime, the ANC and Inkatha have been bitter opponents for many years.

There were also a few critics of apartheid in the all-white parliament. Helen Suzman had served as a member of parliament in South Africa since 1953. She joined the Progressive Party (later to become the Progressive Federal Party) when it was formed in 1959 and earned an international reputation as a courageous and outspoken defender of civil rights. Other opponents of apartheid included a liberal white women's organization called the Black Sash which was founded in 1955; composed mainly of English-speaking women, the Black Sash undertook many silent vigils in protest against the numerous National Party laws passed after that date.

Throughout the 1970s and 1980s black resistance made it increasingly clear that the white government's apartheid policies were failing. In order to quell town-

It is crazy for the government not to take advantage of his [Mandela's] position of authority among blacks, authority which I believe he would use to the benefit of all South Africa. I believe Mr. Mandela's talents should be used before it is too late and far more radical elements take control of the ANC.

Helen Suzman, following a prison visit to Nelson Mandela, May 1986.

ship unrest, the government had to call a state of emergency and maintain repression at an extraordinary level. Through the Suppression of Communism Act, the Terrorism Act, and the Internal Security Act, the state could hold people without trial, keep them in solitary confinement, ban political organizations, hold people under house arrest, exile them to rural backwaters, stop political meetings, and censor the press. Between 1963 and 1990 more than eighty people died in police custody in suspicious circumstances. During the states of emergency between 1985 and 1989 over 40,000 people were detained and more than 1,000 killed by the security forces. The state was prepared to use repression to overcome uprisings but it could not continue to do this indefinitely.

Young people taunt the police in 1981, on the fifth anniversary of the Soweto uprising. The 1976 uprising started as a children's war and occurred mainly in the townships, but the 1984-86 unrest was far more widespread and involved children and adults from the remoter communities as well as the townships.

CONSTITUTIONAL REFORM

During P. W. Botha's presidency (1978–89) the government adopted the total strategy doctrine (see page 38) on the one hand, while on the other it embarked on the reform of apartheid. In 1986 certain "outdated" laws were dropped, namely the Immorality Act and the Prohibition of Mixed Marriages Act. The hated passes were also abandoned. The constitution was reformed to give coloreds and Indians more political rights. In the mid-1980s scenes of violence in the townships intensified calls for sanctions by the international community and increased South African isolation. There were still some Afrikaners who clung to a rigid belief in the separation of the races – in response to the constitutional reforms, fourteen National Party members left to form the Conservative Party – but they were a minority. Most whites accepted that they could not continue to live in isolation.

Another nail in the coffin of apartheid was supplied by the organized resistance of black trade unions. As more black workers were recruited to skilled jobs in the mines and factories, their trade unions' bargaining power with employers increased. In March 1973, 50,000 Durban workers went on a series of strikes.

Striking coal miners chant "Viva ANC" ("Long live the ANC") outside Matla coal mine in 1987, after clashes with security guards firing rubber bullets left six miners injured.

During the Soweto uprising there were many strikes, including a one-day general strike in May 1986 and a national gold and coal strike of over 220,000 miners in August 1987. In June 1987 the railroads were brought to a halt when 16,000 railroad workers went out on strike. South Africa needed skilled black workers, and withdrawal of their labor could badly damage the economy. In December 1985 the Congress of South African Trade Unions (COSATU) was launched and it joined the United Democratic Front (UDF) in the Mass Democratic Movement (MDM), which opposed the government's policies.

The final blows to apartheid came with the 1985 financial crisis (when foreign banks called in their loans), with the increase of sanctions, and with the recession of the late 1980s. The collapse of Communist governments in Eastern Europe in 1989 signaled that the fear of communism was no longer a valid reason for Western governments to support South Africa.

A PRELUDE TO DEMOCRACY

In September 1989 F. W. de Klerk took over as leader of the National Party and state president. De Klerk announced that since the votes cast for the National and Democratic Parties totalled 70 percent, he had a mandate for change. In October he released eight high-ranking political prisoners, including Walter Sisulu. On February 2, 1990, de Klerk declared that "the time for talking had arrived," and announced that his government would try to create a new South Africa. He lifted bans on thirty-two political organizations, including the ANC, PAC, and South African Communist Party. Within ten days Nelson Mandela was freed after more than twenty-seven years in prison. Happiness reigned in the townships.

Over the next two years the pillars of apartheid legislation were demolished. In 1990 the Suppression of Communism Act and the Separate Amenities Act were repealed. In 1991 the Group Areas Act, Population Registration Act, and the Bantu Education Act all went. In that same year the notorious 1913 Native Land Act and the 1936 Act that succeeded it were also repealed. But the end of apartheid had to signify more than the dismantling of laws that had given formal approval to a system of white dictatorship. If apartheid was truly to be pronounced dead

In 1990, when it was announced that Nelson Mandela would be released on February 11, I broke out into a dance, I did the 'toyi-toyi'. Only so could I give vent to all that I felt, all that I knew our people felt.

Archbishop Desmond Tutu of Cape Town, in Joseph Harker's The Legacy of Apartheid, *1994.*

Our idea of an interim government of national unity is that it should be based on the principle that a party which emerges as the strongest in a general election should form the government. But we believe that the problems of our country can only be properly addressed if the majority party invites other parties to join the government of its free will, not because it is forced by the constitution.

Nelson Mandela, ANC leader, 1993.

45

The release of Nelson Mandela, seen here with his (now estranged) wife Winnie, on February 11, 1990, was a landmark in the struggle against apartheid. Mandela had spent twenty-seven years in jail. As a free man he was able to lead the ANC in its negotiations with the government.

then power had to be handed over to a government democratically elected by all South Africans. There followed lengthy negotiations between the government and the ANC to work out a new constitution for South Africa.

There were other signs of normalization of life in South Africa. Some of the 3,000 political prisoners were freed in 1990 and those in exile were given an amnesty and allowed to return. ANC president Oliver Tambo returned to his home country in December 1990. The death penalty was suspended for all but major crimes, and press censorship was relaxed. In June 1990 the South African government ended the four-year state of emergency in all provinces except Natal, where fighting between ANC supporters and Inkatha persisted. Strangely, one major consequence of the repeal of apartheid laws was an upsurge of violence in the townships as rival factions settled old scores and fought for a say in the new South Africa.

There were clashes between Inkatha and ANC supporters in the Transvaal as well as in Natal. In the first six months of 1992, 1,500 people were killed in such incidents. There were also random attacks on commuters from Soweto to Johannesburg and violence in remoter rural areas. Finally, in October 1992, the state of emergency was lifted in Natal province.

The talks about South Africa's future continued haltingly. In December 1991 the government called the first Convention for a Democratic South Africa (CODESA). De Klerk then decided he needed a formal mandate from white people to continue the negotiations, and called for a vote to be held in March 1992. Some 68 percent of voters showed their support for the negotiations to end white minority rule. On March 17 de Klerk announced that: "Today we have closed the book on apartheid."

In September 1992 Buthelezi and the Inkatha Freedom Party withdrew from CODESA after the government had reached an understanding with the ANC. In March 1993 the talks between South African political groups about South Africa's future resumed after a nine-month break. Various agreements were reached on the transitional arrangements leading up to free and fair elections. However, the agreements were

Zulu workers brandish traditional weapons outside their hostel in Alexandra township in 1991. There has been much tension between Zulu migrant workers (often Inkatha supporters) and township residents, who mainly support the ANC. Attacks on township residents have frequently been blamed on Zulu migrant workers.

Until his assassination in 1993, Chris Hani (pictured here) was thought of as a likely candidate to succeed Nelson Mandela as ANC leader. After his death many feared the outbreak of civil war.

It is crucial that the process [negotiations] is not allowed to slow down. We're facing a regime which, for all its deep crises, has not been defeated. The powers of the security forces are intact and their strategy is destabilizing us by low-intensity warfare. The state orchestration of violence is indisputable.

Chris Hani, secretary general of the South African Communist Party, February 1993.

threatened when right-wing Afrikaners used violence to express their opposition to change. In April 1993 Chris Hani, a senior leader within the ANC-South African Communist Party alliance, was assassinated. A Polish immigrant, Janusz Walusz, and a South African Conservative Party member, Clive Derby-Lewis were later tried and convicted of his murder. There was great anger in the townships and for a while it looked as if there might be a full-scale civil war. In that same month Oliver Tambo, the veteran president of the ANC, died and Nelson Mandela, who had already been the leading ANC negotiator in the talks about South Africa's future, took his place.

The eruption of violence put a strain on relations between de Klerk and Mandela. Mandela talked of the "hidden hand" behind the violence and accused the security forces and right-wing extremists of involvement. The ending of the state of emergency had also brought an end to press censorship and in 1991 newspapers revealed that, in 1989 and 1990, Inkatha had been secretly funded by the South African government via the security police. There were reports of security forces training Inkatha recruits. All of this worsened the already poor relations between the ANC and Chief Buthelezi, who in 1993 signaled his opposition to the post-apartheid future by entering an umbrella organization covering a wide range of groups, known as the Freedom Alliance, with white right-wing extremists. These groups were united in their fear of a deal between the government and the ANC.

The government set April 27, 1994, as the date for the first free, democratic elections to be held in South Africa. It was also set as the date by which the "independent" homelands would be incorporated into South Africa once again. The wider world responded very positively to these developments but was cautious about ending sanctions until it was certain that the new democracy in South Africa was permanent. In October 1993 the United Nations responded to Nelson Mandela's request that economic sanctions against South Africa be lifted. Oil sanctions were lifted in

Oliver Tambo, Nelson Mandela, and Walter Sisulu, with Kenneth Kaunda of Zambia pay their respects at the funeral of Chris Hani. Within five days, Tambo himself was dead from a stroke. He had led the ANC for more than thirty years, most of that time in exile.

Peaceful transition to black majority rule in South Africa has been marred by violence in the townships. In 1991 a young girl from Mandela Park squatter camp outside Johannesburg stands at the barbed wire erected to separate one warring faction from another.

December that year and in May 1994 the UN Security Council lifted its embargo on arms sales to South Africa. In May 1994 South Africa rejoined the Commonwealth and in June 1994 Alfred Nzo, the foreign affairs minister, reclaimed South Africa's seat in the UN General Assembly. South Africa has joined the Organization of African Unity and clearly intends to play a greater role in African affairs. At the end of June 1994 Mandela agreed to help try to end the civil war between supporters of UNITA and the MPLA government in Angola. Both Angola and Mozambique have suffered from long civil wars, made more violent by covert South African aid. The cost of these wars has been 1,000,000 dead in Mozambique and 500,000 dead in Angola. However, South Africa is not currently in a position to do much to help rebuild these countries, as it has first to resolve its own internal problems.

A MORE JUST SOCIETY?

On May 10, 1994, Nelson Mandela, president of the African National Congress, was sworn in as president of South Africa, or as he described it in his inaugural speech: "as the first president of a united democratic, non-racial and non-sexist South Africa." The ANC had achieved a notable victory in the elections by securing 62 percent of the valid votes cast. The National Party won 20 percent of the vote, Inkatha 10 percent, the Freedom Front (the new Afrikaner right party) 2 percent, the Democratic Party 1.7 percent, and the Pan Africanist Congress 1.2 percent.

Nelson Mandela takes the oath of office on May 10, 1994,to become South Africa's first black president. In his inaugural speech he called for the healing of wounds and for national reconciliation.

A NEW SOUTH AFRICA

One of the most surprising aspects of the end of apartheid has been the relatively peaceful transformation of government from a white minority to one of national unity. On November 17, 1993,the ANC, the de Klerk government, and other political parties had finally agreed on an interim constitution under which elections could be held. It provided for two houses of parliament: the National Assembly (consisting of 400 members) and the Senate (consisting of 90 members). It was unclear whether the alliance formed by the right-wing Afrikaners and the Inkatha Party would take part in the elections. At the last minute the more extreme Afrikaner nationalists broke away from the alliance and formed the Freedom Front. Drawing further members from the Conservative Party, the Freedom Front prepared for the elections. A week before the elections were held, Chief Buthelezi finally agreed to take part, and Inkatha's name was added to ballots throughout the country.

The interim constitution is to be replaced by a final one drafted by the two houses of parliament by April 30, 1996. Current arrangements provide for a government of national unity for five years, which means that all parties with a significant number of seats can participate in government. As a result, Chief Buthelezi of Inkatha is minister of home affairs, Thabo Mbeki of the ANC is first deputy president, and F. W. de Klerk of the National Party is second deputy president. The constitution includes a number of clauses righting old apartheid wrongs: the restitution of dispossessed land rights, the right to choose a place of residence, freedom of speech, no detention without trial, and freedom of movement. It includes clauses outlawing discrimination on the grounds of sex, race, ethnic or social origin, sexual orientation, age, disability, religion, conscience, belief, culture, or language. South Africa is now divided into nine provinces: Gauteng, Northern Transvaal, North West, Eastern Transvaal, OFS (Orange Free State), KwaZulu-Natal, Northern Cape, Western Cape, and Eastern Cape. There are eleven official languages: Afrikaans, English, Ndebele, Pedi, Sotho, Swati, Tsonga, Tswana, Venda, Xhosa, and Zulu (the last nine all belonging to the Bantu language group).

The National Executive or cabinet is led by the president, who is elected by the National Assembly.

My fellow Africans, today we are entering a new era for our country and its people. Today we celebrate not the victory of a party, but the victory for all the people of South Africa. The hour that the South Africa we have struggled for – in which all our people be they African, coloured, Indians or white, regard themselves as citizens of one nation – is at hand.

President Nelson Mandela, shortly after being elected president by the National Assembly, May 9, 1994.

The president is accountable to parliament and is bound to act within the constitution. The cabinet consists of the president, two deputy presidents, and up to twenty-seven ministers. Any party with at least twenty seats in the National Assembly can nominate a minister. The president decides what post the party nominee will hold.

The constitution provides for an independent judiciary, and has created the post of public protector and an independent eleven-member Human Rights Commission. This Commission has been set up to investigate government incompetence and abuses of power. There are also provisions for the running of the provinces, granting them self-determination and control over some taxation, laws on agriculture, education (except for higher education), health, conservation, transportation, and police.

These constitutional controls should ensure a fairly smooth political transformation. There is still a question mark over Chief Buthelezi's role in the new South Africa, given his initial pronouncement that he would not participate. In March 1994 an independent inquiry revealed that three senior police officers had allegedly been implicated in supplying weapons to Inkatha in order to disrupt the national elections. The investigations into these allegations continue. But with 10 percent of the vote, Buthelezi's position in KwaZulu-Natal is safe and Inkatha controls the provincial government.

Chief Buthelezi has long been one of South Africa's most influential black leaders. He is now minister of home affairs in Mandela's government. Buthelezi's Inkatha party still dominates in the province of KwaZulu-Natal.

KEEPING THE PEACE?

A major question is: will the new constitutional arrangements do anything to quiet the township unrest? It is thought that some 18,000 people have died during the last ten years of violence in South Africa. In March 1994 the independent Human Rights Commission recorded 266 political killings in Natal, the highest monthly toll during the three months it had monitored events there. President de Klerk responded by declaring a state of emergency in the new province of KwaZulu-Natal. In addition to the strife between ANC and Inkatha there is a history of hostility between the many prosperous Indians (Hindu and Muslim) and the poorer black Africans in Natal, dating back to severe conflict between Zulu and Indians in the Durban riots of 1949. The people of Natal and the townships have grown up surrounded by violence; there is a very high crime rate in the townships and domestic violence is widespread. Many young people

This [Zulu territory] is a region where we dominate. No foreign forces shall come into it to rule over us. No government has ever won the kind of war against opposition which an ANC-Communist Party government will have to wage against us if we resist the present interim constitution.

Chief Mangosuthu Buthelezi in an interview published in The Guardian *in January 1994.*

On April 19, 1994, Nelson Mandela and Chief Buthelezi shake hands as President F. W. de Klerk looks on. All three had just signed an agreement allowing the Inkatha Freedom Party to participate in South Africa's first multiracial elections.

have no future to look forward to: they have endured terrible psychological damage, missed out on education because of school boycotts, and have few job opportunities. These are the consequences of apartheid that the new government will find difficult to deal with.

Another area of change for the new government will be the reorganization of the military, the police, and the civil service. To ensure stability, the ANC has promised to guarantee the jobs and pensions of more than 200,000 civil servants, police officers, and soldiers. Mandela has said that he intends to remove those police officers and covert units responsible for directing assassinations against ANC members and supplying Inkatha fighters. More black policemen will be recruited and some will be put into positions of authority. The national police force will have to be integrated with the homelands police, which was separate under apartheid. The long-term intention is to establish community policing programs at police station level. But the police are resisting change and this may lead to problems especially when dealing with township violence.

The army, said to be 67,000 strong in 1993, will have to be reorganized from a white-dominated body into an integrated national defense force. It will have to incorporate Umkhonto fighters, some 12,000 returning from the frontline states, yet it will need to be cut back as the ANC has said it intends to reduce defense

Mourners walk past the coffins of nine people thought to have been killed by Inkatha supporters in Natal. In the first two weeks of April 1994 the violence in Natal claimed 200 lives, even though a government-declared state of emergency was in force.

spending so that it can allocate more money to the welfare of the people. The new government must work on these problems and be seen to be acting lawfully and with fairness. A 1993 ANC investigation concluded that some Umkhonto members had abused prisoners held in camps in Angola, Uganda, and Tanzania. There were calls from opponents of the ANC, demanding that the guilty should not be rewarded with places in government. The ANC still needs to address this human rights problem by revealing details of the investigations and taking the guilty to task.

The civil service, which the new government inherited from the apartheid system, used to employ some 1,200,000 people to service the different apartheid institutions. The Public Service Commission has the task of restructuring the civil service. The three-house parliamentary system set up by P. W. Botha in 1983–84 and the homelands bureaucracies will have to be reorganized by management teams appointed by the new government. A new Code of Conduct is to be drawn up to ensure that the new civil service is non-partisan, career-oriented, and representative of the whole South African community. There will even be provision for pensions for those who made sacrifices to remove apartheid and achieve democracy.

AFRIKANER RESISTANCE

Another consequence of the end of apartheid that the new government faces is the dissatisfaction of the Afrikaner right wing. Many Conservative Party supporters want their own homeland (*volkstaat*). General Viljoen, the Freedom Front leader and a former chief of the South African Defense Force, has drawn up plans for an Afrikaner homeland made up of 15 percent of South Africa. However his party received only 2 percent of all votes cast in the national elections. The new government will have to consider these demands. If it accepts the notion of an Afrikaner homeland it might lead to splits in the ANC alliance but, if it turns it down, the Afrikaner extremists may well use violence to try and achieve their aims. It is possible that the government may agree to a form of limited self-government at a local level. There are a number of small right-wing extreme Afrikaner nationalist groups, of which the Afrikaner Resistance Movement (AWB) led by Eugene Terreblanche is the largest. But

Eugene Terreblanche and AWB supporters disrupt a National Party rally in 1986. With its pseudo-swastikas, the AWB draws some of its inspiration from the German Nazi Party. Its members include factory workers and crop farmers who feel threatened by the prospect of losing their jobs to blacks.

currently the extreme right is in a state of confusion. In March 1994 the AWB sent a support group to Mmabatho to stop the Bophuthatswana homeland regime from collapsing. Three of its members were shot in cold blood by a Bophuthatswana policeman. The incident was documented, showing the AWB's military unpreparedness, and proving to be a profound psychological shock to the movement. However, as Professor David Welsh of the University of Cape Town has said: "A thwarted, frustrated right, who are prepared to take arms, can do untold damage." It is difficult to estimate how many Afrikaners would be willing to take up arms. There are eighty-seven town councils reluctant to become integrated into the new South Africa and they may choose not to pay taxes, or to instigate some other nonviolent means of resisting change. Terreblanche constantly threatens violence and some of his associates were arrested following bombings prior to the 1994 elections. In a speech at the time he said: "We are Boer people! We are fighters! I think there will be more explosions and more actions if the government ignores the just claim of my people who demand some land."

In the interests of national unity, one of the first actions of the new government has been to announce an amnesty for political prisoners. It has also freed some right-wingers imprisoned for committing atrocities in the past. Some have been excluded from this amnesty, including the murderers of Chris Hani. The justice ministry has set up a two-year Truth Commission to look into crimes committed against humanity by all parties between 1960 and 1993. It will allow victims and perpetrators the opportunity to give their version of events.

TACKLING POVERTY

Apartheid has left a ghastly legacy. There is a horrendous housing shortage and high unemployment; health care is inaccessible and not easily affordable by the majority; Bantu education has left us with a massive educational crisis; there is gross maldistribution of wealth. There is need of healing, of rehabilitation, of confession, of forgiveness, of restitution and reconciliation. Our beautiful land yearns for healing.

Archbishop Desmond Tutu in Joseph Harker's The Legacy of Apartheid, *1994*

Transforming other legacies of apartheid may prove to be more problematic. A just society should provide its people with social and economic rights as well as political and civil rights. This means the provision of decent housing, education, and jobs for the black majority. One of the ANC's electoral pledges was to improve housing and build 300,000 new homes each year. The South African Communist Party politician, Joe Slovo, was originally appointed minister of housing and welfare with responsibility for this program, but he died in 1995 and was succeeded by Sankie Nkondo, the ANC's former chief representative in Germany and Austria. Apartheid has left at least eight million people living in squatter settlements on the outskirts of towns. About twenty-three million people do not have access to electricity, twenty-one million do not have adequate sanitation, and twelve million do not have easy access to water. The ANC's Reconstruction and Development Program includes plans to build one million new homes; it also provides for the electrification of two-and-a-half million existing homes and the supply of clean water to a further million houses. Meeting the expectations of impoverished black South Africans will be costly in terms of both money and time.

The ANC is also committed to improving education facilities. An independent research organization found that 1.7 million children between the ages of six and seventeen do not attend school. To meet this need the country must build 50,000 new classrooms immediately. It is thought there is only a 50 percent literacy rate among black people, which compares badly with much poorer countries like Zambia and Lesotho. There is also a generation of young people who have missed out on education during the past ten years because of school boycotts and the unrest in the townships. They will need training and education if they are to find jobs. In 1991–92 the government spent three-and-a-half times as much on each white child as it did on each black child. Black teachers are neither well-qualified nor well-paid and the pupil/teacher ratio in black schools is double that of white schools. Black schools have a low pass rate in examination results – 40 percent compared to 85 percent in white schools.

There is a huge difference too between health care for blacks and for whites. In 1992 the infant mortality rate per 1,000 live births was a staggering 52.8 for blacks and 7.3 for whites. Preventable diseases, such as those arising from unclean water and poverty, are common in rural areas. The death rate from tuberculosis in South Africa is up to thirty-five people per day. Medical experts predict a dramatic rise in the number of deaths

June 1994, and conditions in the squatter settlements are still very basic. These children try to keep warm against the near freezing temperatures of a South African winter. Their home is unheated and there is no glass in the windows.

from AIDS (Acquired Immuno-Deficiency Syndrome) in the next decade. The birthrate among black people was high at 2.8 percent per year in 1991–92, and the rapidly increasing population puts a strain on both housing and education. To begin to tackle these problems, South Africa needs to build 1,000 or so primary health clinics over the next five years.

The government's ability to create a more just society depends on whether it can promote conditions likely to lead to economic growth and thus create the wealth necessary to lift the majority of South Africans out of poverty. It has achieved something in the laying down of a temporary constitution that guarantees political and civil rights; but the righting of social and economic wrongs will prove more difficult. If this is not achieved with reasonable speed, democracy may come under threat as the frustrated expectations of the black population explode in further violence.

A health care unit at the Alexandra clinic, outside Johannesburg. If infant mortality rates are to fall then clean water must be provided, sewage treated, and a health education program put in place.

REBUILDING THE ECONOMY

The economy the ANC-led government inherited after forty-six years of National Party rule had been in relative decline since the end of the 1960s. In real terms, living standards per person are no higher now than they were in 1966. Taking the most simple view, the end of apartheid was unavoidable given the disastrous effects it had had on the economy, especially after sanctions began to bite in the 1980s. In 1971 Harry Oppenheimer, a leading South African businessman and chairman of the Anglo-American Corporation, commented on the damage that apartheid was doing to the economy: "Prospects for economic growth will not be attained" he said, "so long as a large majority of the population is prevented by lack of formal education and technical training or by positive prohibition from playing the full part of which it is capable in the national development."

Rush hour at the non-European entrance to Johannesburg's main railroad station in 1982. The wealthy "white" high-rise city center can be seen in the background. Today downtown Johannesburg is a multiracial city, where segregation is a thing of the past.

Two boys play rugby in Sandton, a "white" suburb of Johannesburg. During the 1970s and 1980s, it was found that a quarter of the richest 20 percent of South Africans were black. A few blacks bought houses in exclusive white suburbs where possession of wealth sometimes overcame the color bar.

Committed apartheid supporters, such as Verwoerd, had been willing to sacrifice economic growth for the great ideal: the result was that the economy grew in an uneven way. The emphasis was on exporting raw materials and concentrating industry on producing goods for the home market rather than producing for export. In 1990 the mining industry output accounted for a third of exports at $22.5 billion. Goods produced for the home market were protected by tariffs, and so were not competitive with outside products. The government responded to the economic downturn with increased import charges and tight controls on the export of money. Since South Africa's large companies could not invest abroad they started buying up smaller local outfits with the result that six large corporations now dominate South Africa's business world. These were not conditions in which competition or the free market could flourish. Apartheid had created a scarcity of skilled and semiskilled workers, a vast and expensive bureaucracy, an uncompetitive industry, and, throughout the country, an uneven infrastructure of basic facilities like schools, and water and electricity

systems. Over the years there has been a decline in investment, firstly from abroad and later at home. Industry is not buying new equipment and is therefore not geared up for future expansion.

This is not to say that South Africa does not have some economic advantages, especially compared to its neighbors. The South African economy has just emerged from the worst recession in its history, nonetheless it still outperforms all other African nations, with an annual output worth $112 billion. Aside from its lack of oil, South Africa has the advantage of being rich in minerals and is the world's leading producer of gold. It also has access to cheap and plentiful hydroelectric power, producing half of Africa's total electricity output. It has a professional managerial class and relatively modern transportation and communications systems. Its current inflation rate is back below 10 percent after twenty years during which it consistently exceeded that figure.

Strangely enough, liberal economists have found that black people made some economic progress under apartheid. Between 1970 and 1984 average wages for black people doubled, against a 9 percent increase for whites. The black share of the country's wealth increased from 20 to 30 percent. According to informa-

In 1990 most black South Africans were still living in poverty. Here a mother and child in Boksburg sit among their possessions after having been forcibly moved from their home for which they were unable to pay. The majority of black people still live in primitive conditions without access to electricity, water, or sanitation.

The end of apartheid and the dawn of freedom in South Africa has been a climactic moment, and one which the Commonwealth has been proud to play its part in bringing about. The people of South Africa can also count on the support of their fellow Commonwealth members in the great task of reconciliation and reconstruction which lies ahead.

Chief Emeka Anyaoku, Commonwealth general secretary, May 31, 1994.

The children and grandchildren of South Africa should never again know the violence and suffering. To ensure this, South Africa needs a growing economy based on a new trade and industry policy, which will focus on the creation of job opportunities and the strengthening of our manufacturing and export capacity. Our economic programmes will take into account the need for sustainable development which does not destroy our natural resources. To achieve these plans, we need large scale international investment. I call on the international community to join us in building reconciliation, peace and a better life for all South Africans.

President Nelson Mandela, 1994.

tion assembled by the University of Natal's Human Science Research Centre between 1975 and 1991, more than a quarter of the richest 20 percent of South African households were black and incomes in this group were rising faster than in other groups. In spite of these gains most black people live in great poverty. The Development Bank of Southern Africa found that nine million blacks were described as completely destitute. The unemployment rate is currently thought to be 66 percent (or 46 percent if one excludes the two-and-a-half million scraping a living with informal or black-market jobs, that is working unofficially for cash). Only one in ten of those entering the job market for the first time is likely to find a job in the formal sector of the economy.

A PROGRAM FOR THE PEOPLE

During the 1994 election campaign the ANC produced a five-year plan to meet what Mandela called "the basic needs of the masses." The Reconstruction and Development Programme (RDP) set out an ambitious $11 billion plan to create jobs and training opportunities for two-and-a-half million people in public works projects. The government promised to provide free education for children and those who had missed out on education in the last ten years. It also promised to redistribute 30 percent of all farming land to those who had lost their land under apartheid.

For years white people were afraid that if the ANC came to power its commitment to socialism would entail the nationalization, or government takeover, of industry and agriculture. However, the collapse of the Soviet Union and its allies has cooled the ANC's enthusiasm for state ownership and the RDP does not include any plans to take over economic activity or to nationalize industry. In an attempt to reassure business, Nelson Mandela said in 1994: "The Reconstruction and Development Programme is a document based on common sense, and there is absolutely not a single sentence about nationalization."

One problem the government of national unity faces is finding the money with which to carry out the RDP. In his speech to the new parliament in 1994, Mandela promised not to increase taxes during the year 1994–95, ruling out taxation as a possible source of immediate revenue. It has been suggested that the

government might find the money from a kind of "apartheid dividend," that is by getting rid of corruption, cutting down the apartheid bureaucracy, cutting defense spending, and collecting taxes more efficiently. Can the government raise money for the RDP from other sources? Now that sanctions have been lifted, there is hope that investment money may come from abroad, creating new jobs and increasing economic growth. Since the end of 1989 some 150 foreign companies have opened up in South Africa. Development experts say the economy needs to grow by well over 3.5 percent if new jobs are to be created; but early in 1994 the International Monetary Fund predicted that South Africa's economy would grow by only 2 or 3 percent, so this looks a little unlikely.

Another way to increase economic growth would be for the government to borrow money or run up a deficit (in other words, to spend over and above its income). De Klerk's government limited its borrowing to 6 percent of the $110 billion gross domestic product (GDP). The ANC has said that it will not keep its expenditure tied to a fixed amount. In 1993 government spending was already quite high at 20 percent of GDP (it was 15 percent in 1983).

An open-air school, some 15 miles from Johannesburg in 1987. Black teachers have often had to run schools on shift systems because there are too few pupil places to satisfy demand. Improving existing educational facilities will be a major item of government expenditure.

We say the economy of this country must be built on sound market principles.

President Nelson Mandela, 1994.

Thabo Mbeki, South Africa's first deputy president, has spent twenty-eight years in exile. During that time he was a foreign envoy for the ANC and built a reputation for diplomacy. He will need this skill if he is to coax money from foreign governments to fund the ANC's Reconstruction and Development Program.

[We need training and public works] focusing on those kinds of elements that would equip young people with a set of fairly portable core skills, allowing them to be much more easily absorbed into a highly productive work force. I see public-works programmes not as a panacea for job creation but as a stepping stone to labour absorption, which is a problem in this country.

Trevor Manuel, head of the ANC's Department of Economic Planning, April 1994.

There will undoubtedly be more aid available from abroad. The United States has promised $90 million and this may be increased to $175 million – a large amount, but a mere drop in the ocean of the needs of the RDP. When South Africa was welcomed back into the British Commonwealth on May 31, 1994, promises of aid were made. It remains to be seen whether countries in Europe, still dogged by the recession of the early 1990s, will increase aid to South Africa. Thabo Mbeki, the deputy president, has expressed the hope that South Africa will receive increased amounts of aid from friendly governments: "It will be very good if we can generate a billion dollars from around the world that can go into projects that will produce relatively quick results [so that we can get] commitments to enable us to build 50,000 houses within a short period without additional government borrowing or raising taxes."

Another question facing the government is how to control black peoples' demands for higher wages. It cannot afford to pay civil servants more if it is to fund the RDP. Jay Naidoo, the general secretary of COSATU, the leading trade union organization, has joined the government as minister without portfolio and one of his tasks may be to ensure that trade union demands are kept in line.

South Africa needs a period of stability to revitalize its economy and restore business confidence in the future. If the government can bring peace to the townships it will be halfway there. Mandela has talked about bringing in tough gun control laws to curb the violence. Overall the outcome of the 1994 elections has given the people of South Africa hope that life will improve. But the government faces the daunting task of rebuilding the economy in the knowledge that it may take twenty years, or longer, to undo the consequences of apartheid.

Resolving violence has to link our programme of rebuilding this country and our ability to raise the standard of living. Because a lot of that criminal violence is a consequence of poverty.

Jay Naidoo, general secretary of COSATU, April 1994.

Children in Soweto pray for peace. They have grown up amid unrest, insecurity, and poverty. The end of apartheid has, however, brought them hope for the future.

CONCLUSION

It would be a mistake to view South Africa exclusively through its background of apartheid. In many ways the problems facing the country, although made more severe by apartheid, are similar to those faced by many developing countries. South Africa needs to develop its industry and provide employment for its citizens. It needs decent, affordable housing and the infrastructure that goes with a modern society: roads, water systems, and electricity lines. The collapse of apartheid has coincided with a sharp rise in violent crime, drug trafficking, and pornography, confirming that the government must lose no time in addressing the problem of poverty. Oddly, one of the consequences of the end of apartheid is that in the immediate future not much will change. It will take years, if not decades, to undo the wrongs that were done. The economy will probably be slow in recovering and it will take a long time for the gap between rich and poor, white and black to be reduced.

One of the fears of the white minority has been that of impending civil war. They have seen neighboring African countries such as Angola and Mozambique ravaged by years of intense fighting. Even in Zimbabwe the progress to independence was accompanied by considerable violence. In some ways South

The lack of adequate drainage facilities means that a wet winter can cause havoc for poorer people in South Africa. Here at Crossroads squatter camp near Cape Town a resident digs a trench to drain water from flooded homes.

In September 1994 some 300 children and parents marched through Bosmont, a mixed race township near Johannesburg, demonstrating against drug dealers. The increase of trade in illegal drugs is a problem yet to be resolved by the South African government.

Africa faces the same problems as Zimbabwe did in 1979: the need to maintain agricultural production, to redistribute land, and to reduce the gap between rich and poor. But it has a major advantage over Zimbabwe, where a huge number of skilled white workers left the country when independence was declared (many of them moving to South Africa), making it difficult to maintain industrial production. Most whites in South Africa have stayed on – they have nowhere else to go – but the majority believes that it is in their interests to make the new South Africa work.

Sometimes African problems can look almost incurable to Western eyes: recurring droughts and famines in Ethiopia, endless wars in Angola and Mozambique, civil wars between Hutus and Tutsis in

When you want to get a herd to move in a certain direction you stand at the back with a stick. Then a few of the more energetic cattle move to the front and the rest of the cattle follow. You are really guiding from behind. That is how a leader should do his work.

President Nelson Mandela, 1994.

Rwanda. Democratic institutions have not had much success in post-colonial Africa, military coups are relatively frequent and there are a number of military regimes currently in power. South Africa has for the last forty years tried to cut itself off from the rest of the continent and its problems, but it must now redefine its relations with Africa and perhaps provide a model for democracy and economic growth.

A RAINBOW NATION

Mandela is an appealing and magnetic leader with a strong desire for peace. His talents for diplomacy and restraint are reflected in his conciliatory attitude to his former enemies.

A big question mark hangs over the ANC – will it be able to put its policies into practice and keep all its allies satisfied? Coalitions can be subject to rapid change: for example, the Civic Forum that came to power after the Communist collapse in Czechoslovakia lasted only a few years before separating into political parties of the right and center. Under the strong lead-

ership of Nelson Mandela, there is hope that the ANC coalition will remain intact. He needs to improve relations with Chief Buthelezi and keep South African Communist Party and trade union support. Of major concern is Mandela's age – he was 77 in 1995 – and his stamina. Mandela supports efforts at friendship and harmony and, as he said on May 10, 1994, "a rainbow nation at peace with itself and the world." Let us hope he can achieve this aim and heal the wounds left by the years of apartheid.

A mixed race school in Cape Town. Hope for the new South Africa means that children will grow up without the injustice of segregation.

GLOSSARY

Afrikaans
The language of the majority of white South Africans. It evolved from Dutch.

Afrikaners
White South Africans of mainly Dutch descent.

apartheid
An Afrikaans word meaning apartness. It is used to describe the system of law which segregated whites and nonwhites.

banned
Under apartheid, political parties were declared illegal by banning. People could also be banned. This meant that an individual could not meet with more than one person at a time and had to live at a designated address.

Boer
The Dutch or Afrikaans word for farmer. It came to be used for the Dutch settlers in South Africa or for the Afrikaners as a group.

bureaucracy
The administration of government through departments managed by sets of appointed officials.

coalition
The union of a number of political parties or factions.

Cold War
A period of strained relations between the United States and the Soviet Union after 1945. It lasted on and off until about 1988.

colored
An apartheid term used to describe those officially classified as of mixed race, including descendants of the Khoikhoi and the San as well as of the Cape Colony slaves.

communism
A political belief based on ideas developed by Karl Marx. He held that the state should own all the factories, land, and mines on behalf of the people.

conservative
A term used to describe a person or organization inclined to oppose change and to support conditions as they exist. In South Africa it applied to those who supported continuing the policy of apartheid.

democracy
A political system in which everyone registered has the right to vote. The government is ruled by the people through elected representatives.

economist
A specialist in economics, the science that deals with the production, distribution, and consumption of wealth.

frontline states
Those states neighboring South Africa, including Botswana, Angola, Namibia, Zimbabwe, Mozambique, and others.

GDP
Gross domestic product – the total national output of a country less its income from abroad.

homelands

An apartheid term for the original native reserves. The word implied that all black people originated from rural homelands, the only places where they were permitted civil rights. Blacks working and living outside their homelands had to carry homeland passports, and were not counted as South African citizens.

ideology

A body of concepts that constitute the thinking behind a political or economic system.

Indians

The descendants of Indian citizens, many of whom arrived in South Africa from India during the nineteenth century.

Marxist

A follower of Karl Marx (see **communism**).

minister without portfolio

A government minister without any specific office, or area of concern.

pass

A document officially known as a reference book, which until 1986 had to be carried by all black people over the age of sixteen. It showed whether the holder was legally allowed in a "white" area.

recession

Economic downturn.

right wing

Similar to conservative; opposing socialism.

socialism

Political ideas developed in the nineteenth and twentieth centuries which emphasize equality and social welfare.

Soviet Union

The Union of Soviet Socialist Republics, a Communist state formed in 1922, dissolved in 1991.

superpower

A term used to describe a very powerful nation, usually taken to mean the United States or the former Soviet Union.

tariff

A system of taxes placed by a government upon imports.

total strategy

A policy adopted in 1978 by the South African government involving the total economic, political, and military mobilization of the state against what it claimed was a Communist onslaught.

white

An apartheid term for all those not classified as nonwhite. Before 1948 whites were called "European." Whites were regarded as one national group, though this group incorporated many national and cultural differences.

World War II

A war lasting from 1939–45. Germany, Italy, and Japan fought against the United States, the Soviet Union, Great Britain, France, Australia, New Zealand and others. South Africa fought as part of the British Empire.

TIMELINE

A.D. 100s — Bantu-speaking farmers begin to enter eastern South Africa. They are the ancestors of present-day South Africa's black population.

1652 — The Dutch East India Company founds a settlement at the Cape of Good Hope.

1795 — Britain takes the Cape Colony from the Dutch.

1803 — The Dutch regain the Cape Colony by treaty.

1805 — The British reconquer the Cape Colony.

1816–28 — The Zulu kingdom is created.

1820 — British settlers arrive in the Cape Colony.

1833 — Slavery is abolished throughout the British Empire. Afrikaner farmers lose their slaves with little compensation.

1834–35 — The British defeat the Xhosa.

1836–37 — Boers leave the Cape Colony in the Great Trek to Natal, the Orange Free State, and the Transvaal.

1842 — Britain annexes Natal.

1852 — Britain recognizes the Transvaal as an independent Boer republic.

1854 — Britain recognizes the Orange Free State as an independent Boer republic.

1868 — Britain annexes Lesotho.

1871 — Britain annexes territory (Griqualand West) where diamonds have been found.

1877 — Britain annexes Transvaal.

1879 — British forces defeat the Zulus.

1880–81 — The Transvaal Boers defeat the British in the First Anglo-Boer War.

1886 — Gold mining begins in the Transvaal.

1890 — Cecil Rhodes is elected prime minister of the Cape Colony.

1899–1902 — The Second Anglo-Boer War leads to Britain conquering the Boer republics.

1910 — The Union of South Africa is formed, uniting the Cape Colony, Natal, Transvaal, and the Orange Free State as a self-governing colony within the British Commonwealth.

1912 — The South African Native National Congress is formed (it is renamed the African National Congress in 1923).

1913 — Native Land Act restricts ownership of land by black people to reserves.

1921 — The South African Communist Party is formed.

1939–45 — South Africa takes part in World War II.

1944 — The ANC Youth League is formed. Its leaders include Robert Sobukwe, Nelson Mandela, Walter Sisulu, and Oliver Tambo.

1948 — The National Party wins the elections. Daniel Malan becomes prime minister. Apartheid becomes official government policy.

1950 — The Population Registration Act and the Group Areas Act are passed. The Suppression of Communism Act is passed. The SACP dissolves and its members join the ANC.

1952 — The ANC and its allies launch a passive resistance campaign.

1954 — Malan retires as prime minister and is replaced by Johannes Strijdom.

1955 — The Congress of the People adopts the Freedom Charter.

1956 — Congress Alliance leaders are arrested for treason but are later found not guilty.

1958 — Hendrik Verwoerd becomes prime minister.

1959 — The Pan-Africanist Congress is formed.

1960 — British prime minister Harold Macmillan visits South Africa and makes a famous speech in which he declares: "the wind of change is blowing through this continent and, whether we like it or not, this growth of national consciousness is a political fact." Police shoot and kill sixty-nine demonstrators at Sharpeville. The ANC and PAC are banned.

1960–83 — Some 3.5 million people are moved from cities to the homelands.

1961 — South Africa becomes a republic and leaves the Commonwealth. Albert Luthuli receives the Nobel Peace Prize. Umkhonto we Sizwe is formed.

1964 — Mandela and other ANC and PAC leaders are given life sentences.

1966 — Verwoerd is stabbed to death. He is succeeded by John Vorster.

1968 — Students form a Black Consciousness organization with Steve Biko as president.

1975 — Mozambique and Angola gain their independence from Portugal.

1976–77 — Mass protests in South African townships lead to hundreds of deaths.

1976 — Transkei becomes the first homeland to be given nominal independence.

1977 — Steve Biko dies in police custody. The United Nations imposes a ban on arms sales to South Africa.

1978 — Vorster resigns. P. W. Botha becomes prime minister.

1980 — Southern Rhodesia becomes independent and is renamed Zimbabwe.

1981–88 — South African forces invade Angola and make raids in Lesotho, Mozambique, Zimbabwe, and Zambia.

1982 — The National Party splits over Botha's proposed constitutional changes. Chief Buthelezi rejects plans to make KwaZulu independent.

1983 — The UDF is formed to resist the new constitutional arrangements.

1984 — Mozambique signs an agreement with South Africa and agrees to expel the ANC from its territory. A new South African constitution gives Asians and coloreds the right to vote for their own legislative bodies. Bishop Desmond Tutu is awarded the Nobel Peace Prize.

1984–86 — Nationwide uprising in South Africa against apartheid.

1984 — Foreign banks refuse to give South Africa any new loans.

1986 — The government declares a national state of emergency during which the security forces have unlimited powers and the press is tightly censored. The U.S. Congress imposes strict sanctions on South Africa.

1988 — SADF troops are defeated in Angola. SADF and Cuban forces agree to withdraw from Angola.

1989 — F. W. de Klerk succeeds Botha as prime minister.

1990 — Mandela and other political prisoners are released. De Klerk lifts restrictions on thirty-three opposition groups. Violence in South African townships continues. Oliver Tambo returns after thirty years in exile.

1991 — The Native Land Acts of 1913 and 1936, the Group Areas Act of 1950, and the Population Registration Act of 1950 are repealed. CODESA talks begin.

1992 — White voters endorse de Klerk's reform policies. CODESA talks end.

1993 — CODESA talks reconvene. Chris Hani is assassinated. The United Nations lifts most remaining sanctions. The transitional constitution is approved. Mandela becomes ANC president. Mandela and de Klerk are jointly awarded Nobel Peace Prize.

1994 — South Africa's first universal suffrage elections held. Mandela is sworn in as president.

FURTHER READING

Brickhill, Joan. *South Africa: the End of Apartheid?* Watts, 1991

Griffiths, I. *Crisis in South Africa.* Rourke, 1988

Harris, Sarah. *Sharpeville.* Trafalgar Square, 1989

Hills, Ken. *1960s,* "Take Ten Years" series. Raintree Steck-Vaughn, 1993

Hoobler, Dorothy and Hoobler, Thomas. *African Portraits,* "Images Across the Ages" series. Raintree Steck-Vaughn, 1992

—— *Mandela: The Man, the Struggle, the Triumph.* Watts, 1992

Leas, Allan. *South Africa.* Trafalgar Square, 1992

McSharry, Patra and Rosen, Roger. *Apartheid: Calibrations of Color.* Rosen, 1991

Miesel, Jacqueline. *South Africa at the Crossroads.* Millbrook, 1994

Omond, Roger. *Steve Biko and Apartheid.* Trafalgar Square, 1991

Pascoe, Elaine. *South Africa: Troubled Land.* Watts, 1992

Paton, Jonathan. *The Land and the People of South Africa.* HarperCollins, 1990

Smith, Chris. *Conflict in Southern Africa.* Macmillan, 1993

Tessendorf, K.C. *Along the Road to Soweto: A Racial History of South Africa.* Macmillan, 1989

Twist, Clint. *1970s,* "Take Ten Years" series. Raintree Steck-Vaughn, 1994

—— *1980s,* "Take Ten Years" series. Raintree Steck-Vaughn, 1994

INDEX

Numbers in *italics* indicate pictures and maps

ACKNOWLEDGMENTS

The publishers are grateful to the following for permission to reproduce photographs:

Cover photo (large): Reuters/Bettmann
Cover photo (small): AP/Wide World

Abbas/Magnum Photos: page 18; Associated Press/Topham: pages 22, 23, 27, 39, 43, 71; Chris Steele Perkins/Magnum Photos: pages 35, 40; Greg English/Link: page 30; Ian Berry/Magnum Photos: page 19; Jillian Edelstein/Link: page 33; Link/ Orde Eliason: page 61; Mary Evans Picture Library: pages 8, 9, 10, 11, 12; Popperfoto: pages 13, 14, 28, 60, 65, 66, 68; Popperfoto/Reuter: pages 54, 55; Popperfoto/UPI: pages 32, 53; Press Association/Topham: page 21; Range/Bettmann/UPI: pages 17, 24, 25; Range/ Reuters/ Bettmann: pages 6, 29, 31, 37, 44, 46, 47, 50, 51, 57, 59, 62, 63, 67, 69, 70; Topham Picturepoint: pages 48, 49; United Nations: pages 16, 20, 41.